"A wonderful manifesto thinking, biblical content page. Every church leade book now!"

**– Gavin Calver, Director of Mission, Evangelical Alliance**

"Ian writes with both passion and understanding. He is passionate about seeing the church of today being like the first church – empowered and fruitful in mission, welcoming and compassionate in its pastoral work, and relevant and transformative in everything. He also writes with the wisdom gained both from his wide reading and from his hands-on local church leadership; he has practised what he preaches. This book is an invaluable toolbox for leaders willing to navigate the turbulent waters of change for the sake of seeing disciples being formed and the church growing."

**– John and Anne Coles, New Wine**

"Ian is someone I have respected and admired for a number of years. His track record as a church leader speaks for itself. He has been a friend, coach and mentor to me and many other young leaders and we have all benefited greatly from his wisdom and experience. Now that wisdom and experience is available to everyone who reads this book. There are insights and strategies here which will interest, inspire and equip you, whatever your leadership role. Ian's humour, wisdom and passion come through on every page. Make sure you read this book if you are in any way involved with leadership in your church – you'll be glad you did!"

**– Revd Kate Wharton, church leader and author**

"Ian Parkinson has vast experience of church leadership and growth within the UK and globally. He knows what he is talking about. This book distils a great deal of valuable wisdom on working in tune with the Spirit to bring about the renewal and revitalisation of the church."
**– Revd Dr Graham Tomlin, Principal, St Mellitus College**

"Many church leaders struggle with turning a church round. This book is a great guide for the process. Clear, full of practical wisdom and theological insight, it takes the reader through re-engineering a church stage-by-stage and encourages those on the journey to keep going."
**– James Lawrence, Leadership Principal, CPAS**

# REIGNITE

Seeing God
rekindle life
and purpose
in your church

IAN PARKINSON

MONARCH
BOOKS

Oxford UK, and Grand Rapids, USA

Published by Monarch Books
an imprint of
**Lion Hudson plc**
Wilkinson House, Jordan Hill Road,
Oxford OX2 8DR, England
Email: monarch@lionhudson.com
www.lionhudson.com/monarch

ISBN 978 0 85721 669 4
e-ISBN 978 0 85721 670 0

First edition 2015

Printed and bound in Great Britain by
Marston Book Services Ltd, Oxfordshire

**Acknowledgments**
Scripture quotations marked NIV taken from the Holy Bible, New International Version Anglicised. Copyright © 1979, 1984, 2011 Biblica, formerly International Bible Society. Used by permission of Hodder & Stoughton Ltd, an Hachette UK company. All rights reserved. "NIV" is a registered trademark of Biblica. UK trademark number 1448790. Scripture quotations marked NLT are taken from the Holy Bible, New Living Translation, copyright © 1996, 2004, 2007 by Tyndale House Foundation. Used by permission of Tyndale House Publishers, Inc., Carol Stream, Illinois 60188. All rights reserved. Scripture quotations marked NASB are taken from the New American Standard Bible®, Copyright © 1960, 1962, 1963, 1968, 1971, 1972, 1973, 1975, 1977, 1995 by The Lockman Foundation. Used by permission. Scripture quotations marked The Message are taken from The Message. Copyright © by Eugene H. Peterson 1993, 1994, 1995, 1996, 2000, 2001, 2002. Used by permission of NavPress Publishing Group.
Quotations pp. 48, 72, 135, 144, 219 from *Relational Leadership* by Walter Wright, copyright © 2000 Walter Wright. Reprinted by permission of Paternoster Press. Brief quotations pp. 52, 53, 81, 146 from pp. 25, 88-89, 176, 207 from *Leaders: The Strategies for Taking Charge* by Warren Bennis and Burt Nanus. Copyright © 1985 by Warren Bennis and Burt Nanus. Reprinted by permission of HarperCollins Publishers. Quotations pp. 50, 62, 75, 77, 82 from *Leading the Congregation* by Shawchuck and Heuser. Published by Abingdon Press, © 1993.Used by permission. All rights reserved. Quotations pp. 55, 101, 109–110 from *The Fifth Discipline* by Peter M. Senge. Published by Random House Business Books. Reprinted by permission of The Random House Group Limited.
Quotations pp. 64, 87–88, 154, 220 from *Hit the Ground Kneeling* by Stephen Cottrell, © Church House Publishing, 2008. Used by permission.
Quotations pp. 96, 101 from *Managing Transitions: Making the Most of Change* 3rd edition by William Bridges, Nicholas Brealey Publishing, 2009. Used with permission. Quotation p. 147 from *Uprising* by Erwin McManus Copyright © 2003 by Erwin McManus. Used by permission of Thomas Nelson. www.thomasnelson.com. All rights reserved.
Quotations pp. 160, 162, 164–65, 180 from *Natural Church Development* by Christian A. Schwarz. Used by permission: ChurchSmart Resources, USA publisher. Quotations pp. 210, 215–216 from *An Unstoppable Force*. Copyright © 2013 by Erwin McManus. *An Unstoppable Force* is published by David C Cook. Publisher permission required to reproduce. All rights reserved.

A catalogue record for this book is available from the British Library

*For Nadine*
*My best friend, constant encourager, and*
*companion in leadership*

# Contents

# Foreword

These days you probably find yourself with less time than ever. Your to-do lists get continually longer, and your inbox fills up more quickly than you can empty it. Everything seems to move at a faster pace, except our ability to keep up. In this fast-paced and complex world, where there are so many voices vying for our attention, many of us have unread or half-read books on our desks or coffee tables.

However, if you have a heart for the church, if you serve in any form of leadership capacity and are concerned about the future of the church, then this book is for you. Stop what you're doing, and take time to capture the wisdom and encouragement in *Reignite*. This is the book that I would love to have written, and the book that I wished I'd had at my disposal many years ago when I began the journey of church leadership. I'm already a better person for having read it. I've been moved to tears, encouraged with the stories of hope and changed lives, and re-energised in my own passion to serve more effectively as a church leader.

I've known Ian, and his wife Nadine, for many years now, as both a friend and a colleague within the New Wine movement. They are a wonderful couple, and Ian is a leader whom I greatly admire, respect and love. In times of great challenge, he is someone who has had a very significant contribution in the life of New Wine and particularly in the north of England. He has encouraged and inspired many, and mentored and raised up lots of younger church leaders.

In times of great challenge and wrestling for the wider church, we need the help of "guides". Ian, in this contribution, is such a guide, helping make sense of the seismic changes happening all around us in our culture, and helping make sense of the call of Jesus to be the church in the 21st century.

*Reignite* is a clear and passionate call to rediscover the purpose of the church. It's a book of great clarity, authenticity, hope and pragmatism. Ian writes to us as one who is uniquely qualified to encourage us all, with insights into leadership, what it means to imagine the future, how to host the presence of God; as well as what it means to lead through transition and to create structures that facilitate and encourage mission and evangelism. You will be opened up to someone whose heart not only beats in tune with Jesus, but to someone who passionately believes that the church is the hope of the world. In investing in this book, you'll be encouraged, envisioned and opened up to the beautiful possibility of what could be. This I believe is a book for the whole church. It will ground new churches as they emerge, and renew older churches, connecting us in a fresh way to Jesus, His call to the church, and the call of the church to the world that Jesus loves and comes to redeem.

Mark Bailey
National Leader, New Wine

# Acknowledgments

**M**any people have contributed, directly or indirectly, to the writing of this book, and I am grateful to all of them for the way in which they have shaped me and thus the pages which follow.

It was from the late Ian Reid, under whose leadership I served on the staff of St Barnabas Church Linthorpe, Middlesbrough, for six wonderfully happy years, that I really learned how to lead an effective local church. The principles I absorbed during those years became the basis for further improvisation when I became senior leader of a church. I am grateful to the members of Emmanuel Saltburn and All Saints Marple, the two churches I have been privileged to serve as vicar, and the two contexts in which the insights expounded in this book have been stumbled upon, tried and tested, for our fellowship in the ministry of the kingdom. I am especially grateful to the many excellent colleagues who are, or who have been, members of our staff team here at All Saints. They have been a source of energy, encouragement, friendship, and inspiration to me over many years, have helped me refine my thinking, have consistently kept me grounded, and have taught me much about the value of team leadership. I hope you know how much I appreciate the privilege of working with you.

The New Wine movement has been the most significant source of encouragement to me for many years and has brought me into contact with so many people whom God has used to shape and develop me. I am especially thankful for my dear friends, who for many years were colleagues on the New Wine National Leadership team, and who have been ahead of me on the leadership journey. I have learned so much about leadership and about growing in leadership from David and Mary Pytches, John and Anne Coles, Mark

Melluish, Mark Bailey, Bruce Collins, and Chris Pemberton. Hanging out with these people has always been an experience of "iron sharpening iron". I am grateful, too, to others who have been fellow travellers along the way, and who have helped me grow in my own leadership in all manner of ways. James Lawrence and Mark Tanner, in particular, have both been, in different ways and at different times, wise counsellors and helpful critical friends. Jed Bartlett has been a huge inspiration in every way!

I must thank the members of the various mentoring groups which I have led in recent years. These groups have been the context in which much of the content of this book has been refined and applied more widely, and also provided the final encouragement to me to put down in written form much of the material I had been teaching for a number of years.

I am most grateful to Jenny Ward at Monarch for the initial encouragement to write a book, and for having sufficient confidence in this project to champion it and enable it finally to be published. The book would be less readable were it not for the efforts of my copy editor, Julie Frederick, who painstakingly polished and improved my original text.

Most of all, I am grateful to my wonderful wife Nadine, who has not only been my greatest encourager for more than thirty years, but also, for most of those years, my closest colleague in ministry. The insights expressed in this book are the result of a journey we have travelled together, and without her I would never have travelled half as far as I have. My appreciation of her is only exceeded by my gratitude to God. I am continually overwhelmed at His grace in inviting me to serve Him and calling me to exercise leadership in His church. Whatever wisdom is contained in what follows is entirely due to Him, and whatever shortcomings are due to the fact that His work in me is still not yet complete.

To Him be the glory.

# Introduction

I believe that the local church is the hope of the world.
I believe to the core of my being that local churches
have the potential to be the most influential force on
planet earth. If they get it and get on with it, churches
can become the redemptive centres that Jesus intended
them to be. Dynamic teaching, creative worship, deep
community, effective evangelism and joyful service will
combine to strengthen families, transform communities
and change the world.[1]

W hen Jesus returned to the Father after three momentous years of ministry on earth, He did so having made careful provision for the continuance and expansion of that ministry of rescue and restoration.

It was a devastatingly simple plan, consisting essentially of reproducing Jesus' own ministry in and through a small community of people. They had not only been shaped through a close relationship with Him, but also now shared precisely His own experience of being filled with the Holy Spirit. That same Spirit – in whose power Jesus operated, and by whose agency working through Him the lost were restored to God, the sick healed, the oppressed set free, and the downtrodden lifted up – was now at work through the lives of Jesus' followers, the church, in exactly the same ways. So clearly did they understand their identification with Jesus and their sharing in His ministry that they came to be referred to as the "body of Christ", the physical presence of Jesus on earth.

No wonder that Bill Hybels can write in such elevated

terms of the unique potential of local churches to be the most significant bringers of hope and transformation in every community. In God's mind they truly are the hope of the world. The tragedy is, however, that at least in the West, influence, hope, and redemptive power are not always the first words that spring instantly to mind when we think of the church. All of us can think of plenty of local churches which frankly seem to be a very far cry not only from this glorious picture that Hybels paints, but equally from the church that Jesus set in motion in the first Christian century.

In her mid-teens, my wife Nadine began to experience real spiritual hunger for the first time. The longing to find answers to life's ultimate questions, the sense that perhaps there might be something more to life than she had thus far discovered, and a desperate desire to find something to fill an inner emptiness led her and a friend to do something they had never done before. They decided to visit a couple of local churches. Neither visit was an especially happy experience. The arcane ritualism of the first left them mystified and perplexed and completely failed to move them or engage with any of their longings. At the second church, lack of any mention of God, and a sermon from the vicar on the different colours of the liturgical year resulted in Nadine sobbing with disappointment, crying out in her heart that, if there was a God, then surely He was interested in deeper things than this!

Having come to the not unreasonable conclusion that the Christian faith clearly had nothing worthwhile to offer, mercifully her decision was swiftly revised when she began to attend a youth club run by another local church. The lives of the Christian youth leaders were impressive and their care and concern for others was winsome. Here was a community that was attractive and that was a living witness to the God who was at its centre. Little wonder that within months Nadine had been helped to personal faith herself and was faithfully nurtured in authentic discipleship.

I am profoundly grateful to that church, for without it I would have never met and married Nadine, would have been denied the satisfaction of decades of life and ministry together, and my own life would have been significantly impoverished! But I can't help wincing inwardly as I wonder how many more seekers over the years have never got beyond sobbing at the back of church, having failed to discover there what they had hoped and expected to find. It's the thought of such people that has, for many years, spurred me on to do what I can to shape the life of the churches I have led in order that they might be most helpful for those who are seeking after God and, indeed, that they might arouse a longing for Him in the hearts of those who are not.

Arguably, communities in the West have never been in more desperate need of the transformative and restorative power that God entrusted to the church for the sake of the world. Challenges such as the rise in family breakdown in many Western nations[2] – with its associated increase in child poverty, ill health, lower educational achievement, and many other negative outcomes – growing rates of treatment for anxiety and depression,[3] and high prison populations[4] all point towards societies that seem broken. Little wonder that more and more broken people, living with the pain of rejection, loneliness, disappointment, fear, and frustration, resort to any and every form of self-medication in order to find some solace and relief.

If ever there was an age in which the church ought to come into its own with its unique offer of new life then this would be it. Tragically, the last thirty years in the UK have seen a 40 per cent decline in the number of people who identify themselves as active members of local churches and a staggering 90 per cent decline among those under the age of twenty![5] This pattern of decline or slowing growth is repeated across much of the Western world. It's not that God's commitment to restoring the least and the lost has in any way changed, or that He has somehow become less able to affect people's lives (in that same period the church in other areas of the world has grown meteorically).[6] Nor is it the case that people today are unwilling to try anything that they think might work to bring them a more satisfying life. Quite the reverse: people today are willing to try anything and everything that holds out some promise!

The simple truth is that in all too many cases local churches have lost the plot. They have lost sight of the lofty destiny and calling of which they are modern-day heirs. Wrapped up in their own domestic concerns, most of which have little if anything to do with their founding purpose, and swept along on the winds of contemporary cultural moods, they have become swamped by the world rather than offering hope to it. Finding themselves on the margins of public life, with an identity as custodians of outdated and largely irrelevant quaint customs and habits, understandably all too many churches have given up on any idea of ever being those who shape and transform a culture as opposed to being shaped by it.

It doesn't need to be like this.

Imagine what our communities could look like if we, the church, were offering hope to those who are desperate or despairing. Imagine if the church was a place filled with possibilities and opportunities. Imagine if our churches so affected our lives and those of our communities that the statistics we saw above, about both church and society, could be fundamentally changed. Could this be a reality?

I believe that it can, and that we can help to see that vision realized.

Churches slip into decline and inertia for all manner of reasons, but the promise of Jesus that He would build His church and that even the gates of hell could not prevail against it[7] still stands as an expression of His determination to have a church which is fit for purpose and pulsates with His life. His own kingdom agenda[8] still burns on His heart, and His strategy for continuing the work He began during His own earthly ministry – a strategy that came into being at Pentecost with the outpouring of the Spirit – remains unchanged. He remains committed to seeing vibrant and vital local churches, dynamic communities of God's life, coming into being in every single community on earth. In many cases this will require the planting of entirely new missional communities, starting from scratch, unencumbered by the baggage, expectations, and disappointments of the past. One of our top priorities as the body of Christ must be to raise up, resource, and release a whole new generation of entrepreneurial leaders who will break entirely new ground for the Christian good news in some of our most fragmented communities. There may be some useful insights for such people in the pages of this book, and some wisdom that might be translatable for those engaged in such enterprises, but this book is not written primarily with church planters in mind.

In many communities, especially those that still have a level of integrity and community identity, there is still scope for a different style of ministry – that of reengineering an existing church and working to see it renewed.[9]

I quite understand those who are now convinced that the only effective strategy for reaching others is to see completely new churches planted from scratch. I understand that the historic churches may seem not only to no longer have the capacity to be retooled for a more missional purpose, but are actually a positive hindrance to the furtherance of such a task and a drain on resources that might be more profitably diverted elsewhere. Contemplating the missional task before us, and looking at the recent track record of denominational churches, might well bring to mind the words of an apocryphal Irishman. When asked by a lost American motorist for directions to Dublin, he scratched his head thoughtfully before commenting that if he were travelling to Dublin, "I wouldn't be starting out from here!"

Nevertheless, there are a number of compelling reasons for seeing the reengineering of such churches as worthwhile. Many denominational churches have clear relational links with their community and with groups and institutions within that community, even if they need to be reactivated. Furthermore, there still exists a level of trust and confidence in a "known brand". Although there may be very little difference in conviction, approach, and ultimately even methodology between new churches and more established ones, the journey to winning people's confidence, and thus a hearing for the gospel, is often shorter for the local vicar than for others. This is perhaps why new churches have tended to plant more successfully in more urban and suburban contexts, and especially among those who are younger and more mobile, where they have the capacity to develop as relational "network" churches rather than as local "community" churches.

There are resources already in place that can be used for kingdom purposes. The chances are that in many traditional churches there will be at least some faithful people who have never really been introduced to a dynamic understanding of Christian discipleship, but who will very quickly come to life and get on board as they are exposed to a new experience of worship, teaching, and ministry in the power of the Spirit. They are the ones who will become a workforce to resource new initiatives.

Buildings can be a decidedly mixed blessing, but it is likely that from the word go there will be a venue at your disposal for events and activities, perhaps also with a house in the heart of the local community. And if a denomination has allocated a salary for the post in question, how much better that it be used to fund a genuinely missional leader than one who will simply maintain a declining status quo!

But the most compelling reason for getting involved in reengineering is a theological one: this is a ministry close to the heart of God. He has a great track record, throughout the history of His dealings with His chosen people, of renewing them in their sense of identity, vision, calling, and anointing. Time and again God's people lose their way, falling foul of the prevailing political and cultural forces, and time and again God brings them back to Himself and to an identification with His great purposes. The last two decades have seen hundreds of churches brought back to life and missional purpose in the power of the Spirit, and the communities that they serve impacted by the power of God, sometimes in quite sensational ways. I have been privileged to see this first-hand and share in it through my involvement with the New Wine Movement in the UK and elsewhere. It is out of this experience, and in the hope that it might offer help to those who are similarly called to a ministry of renewing historic churches, that this book is written.

If this is to happen, then one thing – in addition, of course, to the power of the Holy Spirit – is indispensable. God is looking for those who are prepared to partner with Him in the exercise of leadership and who understand their calling to be agents of change in the church for the sake of the world.

In speaking of those who exercise leadership I do, in part, have in mind those who might be called by God as senior pastors, vicars, ministers, etc., who will find themselves in the position of overseeing local churches. But this book is written with many other people also in mind – people who themselves have a key role to play in the business of seeing transformation come about in the life of local churches. Some reading this book may already occupy leadership positions in your own local church, whether as elders, deacons, church council members, small group leaders, children's leaders, and so on, and thus have the capacity to exercise positive influence for God's kingdom in your existing sphere of ministry. Others may not have a formal leadership position, but a deep desire to see your own church come alive in the power of the Spirit and come to resemble far more the church as God intends it.

One of the vital insights of much contemporary thinking on leadership is the truth that everybody, wherever we find ourselves in the life or structure of any organization, has the capacity to exercise leadership and to contribute to the progress and health of that organization. My hope is that the insights offered in this book will sharpen the focus of many different kinds of leaders and enable us to exercise influence more effectively, no matter what our own unique place within the life of our own local churches. Such transformational leadership comes about when we are gripped by a compelling vision of how God intends His church to be and a passion to do all that we can to move it forward from its current state.

This book begins with a brief overview of the true calling and identity of the church. We go on to examine the catalytic role of leaders in helping others to commit to such a vision and some of the practices and habits that will enable us to see vision become reality. We will consider some strategies for holding our nerve while managing transitions. We will reflect on the vital disciplines of both growing and developing other leaders and of creating functional structures to suit the missional purpose of the church. Most importantly, we will take time to acknowledge that this work of seeing change come about is ultimately God's work, and we explore what it means in practical terms to give space for the Holy Spirit to do His work in and through a local church. And lest we thought that the work of turning a church around was accomplished overnight, our final chapter reminds us that leading such a work is far more a marathon than a sprint and helps us to develop stamina and resilience for the long-haul journey.

As well as expressing some deeply held convictions that have shaped me over more than thirty years as a local church leader, this book is more than anything the fruit of the experience of partnering with God in the reengineering of two very different local church contexts. Along the way I have come across a number of resources which have been incredibly useful to me in this enterprise, and have devised a few more myself. These are appended to the end of relevant chapters in the hope that they may prove equally useful to other readers.

An appendix at the end of the book takes the form of a study guide, a series of questions for further discussion to accompany each chapter. A group of leaders in a local church might helpfully read the book together and then use these questions to apply the material to their own context. Equally, the same exercise could be undertaken by a group of senior leaders of different local churches who might provide mutual encouragement and accountability in the work of bringing about change in the different churches which they lead.

My prayer in writing this book is that it might offer some help for other leaders in terms of identifying and applying some of the key disciplines needed to see churches turned round and begin to impact their communities. I am praying, too, that some who read this book might have rekindled within you a passion to be leaders of change in the situations in which you find yourselves. I pray that God would inspire and encourage you to step up to the calling you have upon your life as He stirs within you the longing for your church to become far more the hope of the part of the world it serves.

# 1

# Recovering Our Identity:
# The Church That God Has In Mind

The Church is the means by which Jesus is uniquely
present and distinctively expresses himself in the world.[1]

When the church is in mission, it is the true church...
The mission of God flows directly through every believer
and every community of faith that adheres to Jesus. To
obstruct this is to block God's purposes in and through his
people.[2]

A missional church is a community of God's people
who live into the imagination that they are, by their
very nature, God's missionary people living as a
demonstration of what God plans to do in and for all of
creation in Jesus Christ.[3]

n early 1992 I accepted an invitation to move to a
small seaside town just south of the Tees estuary on
the edge of the post-industrial north east of England to
become vicar of the only Anglican church in the town. For all
of the 125 years of its history, Emmanuel Church Saltburn
had been a fairly typical "middle of the road" Anglican
church. Recent years had seen it declining numerically and
in influence within the local community from which it was
increasingly disconnected, not helped by a sexual scandal
surrounding my predecessor but one. The modestly sized

congregation had an average age of between sixty-five and seventy and were of a tradition that expected ministry to be the exclusive responsibility of the vicar.

These days they may be smaller numerically, and possibly with congregations whose average age is even slightly higher, but churches like this can still be found in communities in England and elsewhere. Nostalgic for a previous age in which they occupied a far more central role in the life of the community, they tend to be hallmarked by a misplaced optimism which insists that if we just keep doing what we have always done then things are bound to get better one day. They may well be the kinds of churches Ann Morisey had in mind as she reflected:

> *In my more cynical moments I am tempted to think that the mainstream denominations do not lack a theory of Mission. They have a very potent, but implicit, theory of Mission. It is that the church structure, style and location are already appropriately in place. All that is required is that those outside the Church accommodate themselves to what already exists.[4]*

In the week in which I accepted the job, my daily Bible readings "happened" to be from the book of Nehemiah. From that time onwards, Nehemiah became a bosom friend and close companion.

Nehemiah was a member of the Jewish community who had been born in Babylon during the period of exile in the late sixth century BC. A high-ranking official in the court of the Persian emperor — whose antecedent had conquered Babylon and resettled numbers of Jewish people back in their homeland with permission to rebuild their ruined native city — Nehemiah is the leader whom God used as a catalyst finally to see the task of rebuilding achieved.

24

Rebuilding was not simply about restoring the physicality of a once glorious city, but far more about getting the people of Israel back on track with their calling from God to be His representative and missional people on earth for the sake of other nations. It was about a restoration of identity, purpose, and function, about a people becoming once again who God intended them to be.

The parallels with the situation into which I was about to step were uncanny. Events of the recent past had left a number of people emotionally scarred and had winded and demoralized many more, including my immediate predecessor. The image of broken-down walls and accompanying sadness and despair seemed peculiarly apt as I familiarized myself with Emmanuel Church – and not just because of its recent history. There seemed to be a significant mismatch between God's grand vision for His church, His expectation of the role a local church might fulfil, and the assumptions and aspirations that shaped Emmanuel Church's self-understanding and modus operandi. Set right in the middle of a somewhat rundown seaside town, with all the social problems and issues that are so often prevalent in such communities, it didn't seem that the church had any real sense of its call to bring something of the good news of Jesus in word and deed to those who were so lost and broken. There was immense work to be done to help people discover and gain confidence in their true identity and calling in Christ. I was convinced that this was exactly what God wanted to bring about.

I still remember walking round Saltburn that week with a ridiculous sense of excitement and anticipation building within. It wasn't that there was anything about the current state of Emmanuel Church to get the juices going. But the conviction that God was in the business of building His church, and the compelling picture of the church as

Scripture describes it, eclipsed everything else. The next nine years proved to be an exciting adventure of seeing a local church reengineered and begin to resemble far more the New Testament church. It was a project that, I discovered, was very close to God's heart and one that He longs to see replicated in more and more communities.

What was most striking about Nehemiah was that he had very likely never before visited Jerusalem (despite having strong family connections there), let alone seen it in its former glory. His only experience was of destruction and the disappointment which exile had brought. Despite this, Nehemiah never let go of the compelling vision which his Scriptures gave him of God's true purposes for His people. It was this vision of what Jerusalem and Israel might once again become, and a conviction that God wanted to work with him to see this come about, which drove him on and gave him the impetus, against all odds, to see the city rebuilt and Israel rise up once again as God's nation. It was a vision that was so all-consuming it threatened his emotional health, drove him to weep and fast and pray continually over Jerusalem,[5] and shaped the trajectory of his life for the months and years that followed.

If we aspire to be effective agents of change, used by God to reengineer dormant local churches, then we too need to be captivated by a compelling vision of what the church is meant to be and what our church might become, and a restless dissatisfaction with the status quo. Hopefully we will have had first-hand experience of churches that are modelling something of what a functional, kingdom-focused church should look like. I had been fortunate not only to be shaped as a young adult by being part of a pioneering charismatic church in the city where I grew up, but also then to work for six years in a church in Middlesbrough alongside a wonderful colleague who had himself overseen a major reengineering of that church, bringing it into an experience of the ministry of the Spirit and a much more missional identity. My experience in both of these churches had given me not only an exciting picture of what a local church could be like, but also real hope that God could bring such a church into being in the community I was called to serve. I felt I had a basic pattern, not simply to try to impose unreflectively upon my new church, but rather as a basis for fresh improvisation in this new context.

In addition to some experience of seeing such ministry modelled, hopefully we will also have so immersed ourselves in the Bible's narrative that our understanding of God's design for His church and for every local expression of it will be shaped by that narrative.

## WHAT WOULD JESUS DO?

As teenagers, my children could, from time to time, be seen wearing wristbands bearing the acronym "WWJD". It stood, of course, for "What would Jesus do?" and represented a very helpful reminder to strive, in every situation, to be faithful to Him and not to compromise in any way. In my opinion, it's a really good question to ask ourselves and a great way of checking that we are truly on track.

In teenage Christian culture the primary sphere in which faithfulness is sought is in the areas of personal, moral, and spiritual integrity. Perhaps the question "What would Jesus do?" is one whose scope we ought to widen a little more. Perhaps we ought to be asking it about the way in which we "do" church. Perhaps we might rephrase it slightly and ask, "If Jesus were responsible for directing and organizing the local church of which I am part, what would He do?" If Jesus were starting out on His post-resurrection mission today, would He bring into being a church that looks just like our church and organize things exactly the way we are currently doing? How might we go about seeking to discern just what kind of church God has in mind in our own day and age?

When we start asking such a question we find that God has given us some pretty clear answers. In fact, He has spent a good deal of time and effort in seeking to bring about a community of faith which has absolute clarity about its identity and purpose and about God's intentions for it. The clues to such a purpose can be found not only in His interactions with His people Israel in the Old Testament era, but supremely in the ministry of Jesus, in the instructions Jesus gives to the earliest church, and in the spontaneous work of the Spirit in bringing the church into being and directing it in its formative period. And because God's purposes never really change and because the work for which we were created remains unfinished, God, in every generation, is always seeking to renew His church and bring us more into line with those foundational purposes.

In a nutshell, God's church is His primary missional agency, serving His great purpose of partnering with Him in the work of drawing lost people back into relationship with Him – a community called to be a sign and foretaste of what life looks like when God is acknowledged as King.

## A LIGHT TO THE NATIONS

The beginning of God's great work of reconciling a lost humanity to Himself consists in the call of a semi-nomadic Middle Eastern man, Abram, to be the founder of a people who will belong to God in a uniquely close way and among whom God will show His glorious presence and favour. God will pour out His blessing upon them for a very clear and distinct purpose – that they might in turn bless others and be a living sign of God's goodness and truth, such that other nations might in turn be drawn to encounter God and to an authentic experience of His good life.[6] The context in which this great calling was to unfold was challenging. God's truth and light was to be made known to those who were not only far from Him but whose lifestyle and practices were shaped by values far removed from those of God Himself. It is God's love for all those whom He has made, and His concern that all those who are far from Him should be brought back to Him to encounter His presence, that lies behind this strategy and gives shape and identity to the community He calls into existence. From the outset, Israel is called to be a missional people, sent out into the world by and on behalf of a missional God.

Throughout their history, Israel struggles to hold on to this vision of being a people set apart for the sake of others. They enjoy the privileges of being chosen by God but are less attentive to the accompanying responsibilities. Loss of missional purpose has serious consequences. It inevitably leads to complacency and compromise and a tendency to redefine God in order to make Him fit in better with prevailing cultural values. Far from seeking to help the surrounding nations to step out of their spiritual and moral darkness into God's light, Israel adopts many of their pagan practices. The few voices that continue to speak out for the living God are marginalized, ridiculed, and even, at times, destroyed.

Remarkably, despite their gross failure and disobedience, God never gives up on His recalcitrant people. The experience of invasion by a neighbouring superpower and the accompanying destruction of the infrastructure and institutions of their nation gives Israel opportunity to reflect and to turn back to God in penitence. The prophetic literature that emerges towards the end of the exilic period, and in the years immediately after the return of God's people to Jerusalem, is some of the richest in the Old Testament. In it God reminds His people of His own nature and purposes, of the calling of His people to be God's servant on behalf of others and to be a light to other nations.[7] They are to be ministers of God's redemption, healing, deliverance, and restoration throughout the world. Moreover, because of their inability to fulfil such a calling unaided, and because God is so serious in His determination to see His redemptive work fulfilled on earth, God promises to pour out His own Spirit upon every believer in order to cause them to walk in His ways and to enable them to do His will.[8]

Over the course of the next few centuries, Israel's primary concern is that of survival as they are occupied by a succession of different pagan superpowers. Any thought of fulfilling a greater purpose in the world becomes gradually pushed further and further into the future, into an era which will succeed this present age when God will finally establish His unmistakable rule over human affairs. The people who were intended to be God's agency for world transformation have become a tiny embattled minority whose principal concern is to maintain a distinctiveness apart from the rest of the world, and whose defining characteristic is nostalgia for a bygone age when they had greater influence. Sound familiar?

Kenneth is a member of a Pentecostal church in the Serere District of north-east Uganda. Like many such churches, Kenneth's church prided itself on its concern for personal holiness and on the way in which its members refrained from such ungodly pursuits as drinking alcohol (alcoholism is a significant problem in that culture). Kenneth's zeal for Christian distinctiveness led him, from time to time, to visit the local bar where he would berate the regular customers for their drunkenness and explain to them that they were destined to burn in hell. Not only did he not make much headway with his brand of personal evangelism, but his church was very much marginalized and rather despised within the wider community.

A few years ago, Kenneth's church was introduced to the Tearfund-sponsored Church and Community Mobilisation Process,[9] a programme designed to promote sustainable development by helping local churches to work with their communities and to mobilize their own existing resources for the transformation of the community. The process begins with local churches undertaking a series of Bible studies designed to help them gain something of a broader vision for the calling of the local church.

Kenneth was profoundly impacted by this process, especially by the Bible study, which helped him to see that the purpose of the church is to be salt and light to the world. He started visiting the bar more regularly, not to drink, but no longer to berate the customers. He sat with them as they drank. He asked them about their lives, their families, and their challenges. He offered to pray for them. The drinkers understood that Kenneth no longer despised them but rather seemed to have a genuine concern for them.

As the weeks went by, they began to invite their friends along to the bar so that they too might hear some of the stories of God's promises which Kenneth was now relating and also to be prayed for. Gradually, several of these men came to faith in Christ and were set free from addiction to alcohol. Today, those same men are living productive lives, the former bar is now a church building, and that church, of which they were the original members, has planted seven more across the wider community! All because a small, marginalized group of Christians discovered what it truly means to be the church, and reframed their common life accordingly.

Whatever else the Old Testament speaks of, it bears witness to a God who is relentless in His pursuit of lost people, whose love for them and desire for fellowship with them drives Him on, and who thinks that a people who host His presence is the best strategy for revealing Himself to the world. This most basic missional purpose remains the defining feature of the church as God intends it. Any departure from this is to deny God and His purposes for us. It was in order that such a purpose might be accomplished that God made His most radical move.

## MOVING INTO THE NEIGHBOURHOOD

Perhaps the most winsome element of the Christian revelation is the extraordinary truth that God, out of love for lost humanity, entered into our space and time in human form, the Creator becoming part of His creation. In leaving the splendour of eternity and the security of the Father's presence, and in becoming a human being, Jesus demonstrates the lengths to which God will go in His commitment to bringing us back to Himself. He is willing to enter fully into human life and to experience the darkest and most threatening aspects of that life. He is willing even to undergo the most extreme spiritual torment and death as He bears in His own body the eternal consequences of our rebellion against God, experiencing God-forsakenness on our behalf so that we might have opportunity to escape it. He is prepared to lay aside His privileges, to accommodate Himself to us, to get down to our level so that we might be able to see more completely who God is and what He is like.

Some years later the apostle John — one of the eye-witnesses to the life, death, and resurrection of Jesus — reflects on this momentous event. He observes that though no one has ever seen God, the only begotten Son of God became a human being in order to make God known and, as the Message[10] translation of the Bible so beautifully puts it, "moved into the neighbourhood".

God is thus revealed as one who, without compromise to His nature, is prepared to lay aside all that gets in the way of people encountering Him because His primary concern is to seek and rescue lost people. He makes the first move towards us and clothes Himself with the things that are part of our world.

This most fundamental gospel truth has been the driving force behind many contemporary church planting movements, including, in recent years in the UK, the Fresh Expressions initiative. At heart these all represent attempts to allow local churches to come into existence, which are shaped by a missional imperative. In this we rejoice! But it begs the question, is the church truly the church if it is not mission-shaped? If God is a missional God, and if the church is in fact the body of Christ, is it not rather a contradiction in terms, indeed complete nonsense, to contemplate a church that is not missional?

There is a pressing need for the church as a whole, and especially in its more "traditional" forms, to take far more seriously the implications of the incarnation and to critique its practices, rituals, forms, and structures in the light of this most fundamental theological truth. However, nothing ever changes from the top down. Genuine change will only occur from the bottom up as leaders, who are gripped by God and by a vision of what His church is designed to be, work to reengineer churches in accordance with a more biblically faithful pattern.

## SERVANT OF THE LORD

The ministry of Jesus represents not so much a change in God's plans for His people as an intensification of them. Jesus came to fulfil the purposes and destiny with which Israel had consistently struggled. The heart of His teaching about Himself, and the thing that really put the religious establishment of His own day at odds with Him, was His taking of the principal signs and symbols of the Israelite nation and insisting that they were actually fulfilled in Him. He is the true servant of the Lord prophesied in Scripture[11] and has come to perform the acts associated uniquely with that figure.

The vital truth that Jesus comes to announce is that "the kingdom of God has come near";[12] that is, the rule and authority of God, associated with the end of this age, has broken into the present ahead of time. The new age of the Spirit of God, prophesied by Ezekiel, is now here. The prototype Spirit-filled human being has arrived on earth to model what life is to be like for those who, as a result of His ministry, will find themselves as members of the Spirit-filled people of God. Not only does Jesus talk about restoration, healing, deliverance, and experiencing God's favour, but wherever He goes people begin to experience this. It's no surprise there is such widespread awe and wonder from people who have never seen anything like this before[13] and from those who had no idea that God was for them.[14]

When the disciples of John the Baptist are sent by John to ask Jesus if He truly is the messiah (Jesus' approach has caused uncertainty even in the mind of one so unorthodox as John himself), Jesus answers them by referring to the works He is performing, signs that are associated in Scripture with the messiah.[15] What God is about, He is saying, is the restoration of the lost, the healing of the hurt and broken, the setting free of captives, and induction into the realm of God's blessing. And if this is the work of the messiah, then this equally must be the focus of the messianic people who are recruited by Him to share and extend His work.

One of my favourite churches meets each Saturday evening in an old building in the centre of Halifax. Like many former industrial towns, Halifax and its people today have more than their fair share of problems and challenges. Some years ago, a group of local Christians began a foodbank in the town centre. Each week around 150 food parcels are given away to a clientele, a high proportion of whom are either homeless, asylum seekers, victims of abuse, sex workers, addicts or recovering addicts, or who face other significant issues. Not only do those who host the foodbank give away food, but they also give away love; they pray with their clients, and they tell them about the love of God.

As a steady trickle of people began to come to faith, and realizing that none of the existing local churches had the capacity to pastor these new believers, the team established a new church simply called "Saturday Gathering". In 2014 they baptized fifty new believers, and at the time of writing around 100 people meet each Saturday evening for worship, teaching, and ministry and for a hot meal. It is, for me, something of a foretaste of heaven. The church members still face many serious challenges. But they are now facing them with the resources that Jesus provides. This has been possible because a small group of people began to take seriously what it means to follow Jesus, and to do the things He did.

## THE BODY OF CHRIST

Jesus was at pains to make sure that His first followers were left in no doubt about their calling to replicate His own ministry. Having inducted them into the work of the kingdom throughout His time on earth, on His final evening with them, Jesus explains what is to happen when He is no longer physically present. As the Holy Spirit fills and empowers them, they will find themselves doing exactly the same works as He Himself has done.[16] This imperative is underlined by Jesus after His resurrection when He reminds them that they are now being commissioned in exactly the same way that He Himself was commissioned by the Father and to do exactly the same things.[17] Luke unpacks this in greater detail in the opening verses of the Acts of the Apostles. Here, Jesus is described as "giving orders"[18] to the apostles, presumably (given that these orders relate to the kingdom of God)[19] concerning the future shape of the work. This will involve them leaving the comfort of their own place[20] and taking the good news about Jesus and His kingdom even to the ends of the earth.

It is striking to reflect on the meticulous way in which Jesus prepares His disciples for life and ministry beyond His ascension and physical departure from the scene, and on His concern that the church which bears His name should remain within the parameters set by Him.[21] Their faithfulness to this calling is such that Luke makes no distinction between the works they accomplish and those of Jesus.[22] Little wonder that the apostle Paul is later to coin the phrase "The body of Christ" as a description of the church; we are the physical presence of Jesus on earth, indwelt by His Spirit and doing His works. Finally, the story that began with Abram centuries earlier has reached its climax. God has a people for His own possession, filled with His Spirit and demonstrating His life, calling people back to relationship with Him.

## ENDS OF THE EARTH PEOPLE

There is something gloriously uncomplicated about the first Christian community and its self-understanding. With the commission of Jesus[23] still ringing in their ears, and the experience of being filled with the Holy Spirit, the first Christians found themselves turned outwards towards a lost world, with the hope that others would also be moved to embrace Christ and be embraced by Him. Their self-consciousness was of being a missional movement, a sent-out people. Their whole focus was on partnering with Jesus as He sought to extend His mission through the day-to-day encounters His people had with those in their communities.

Jesus' ambition was to see every lost community and every single people group across the earth touched by His presence and coming into an experience of the fullness of life which is found only through relationship with Him. Nothing must be allowed to detract from nor in any way undermine this great enterprise. Domestic difficulties and theological problems, largely to do with the proper place of Jewish tradition in an increasingly racially mixed church, were solved by being considered in terms of their impact upon the pressing missional priorities of the church.[24] Even persecution when it came was seen as providing opportunities to minister in the name of Jesus to new people and in new places.

Summing up the essential identity of the church many centuries later, the great theologian Emil Brunner famously observed, "The Church exists by Mission as fire exists by burning." Here was a community filled with the presence of God, living the life of God, knowing that they existed for the sake of others, and day by day looking for others to welcome in.

This is the church that God longs to see come into being in every community and among every people group on earth.

This is the genius that God wants to see reimplanted into every existing community of believers in every place. The tragedy of the church in large parts of the Western world in recent years is that, largely through its preoccupation with secondary domestic matters or its obsession with preserving outmoded ways of conducting itself, it has lost sight of its core purpose. Instead of, as the first church did so magnificently, allowing its foundational purpose and its missional calling to shape its identity and appearance, the contemporary church in so many places has allowed its identity to be hijacked by a love of nostalgia, and its core purpose to be suffocated by a loss of vision and hope. In many ways it is suffering from amnesia and needs to have restored to it a memory of the true nature of its calling and purposes under God.

It was an understanding of God's purposes and a conviction about God's nature that impelled Nehemiah to undertake a work of rebuilding which most would have seen as both foolish and impossible to accomplish. The key to the success of his enterprise was helping the community of his own day recover their collective memory about God and about their place in His purposes. It was a similar conviction that quickened my spirit back in 1992 and that sustained me, even when the going got tough, as I got stuck into the work of moving a local church out of traditionalism and into an ownership of its kingdom identity and calling.

Many churches today need a complete turnaround in terms of their understanding of what the church is called to be. The role of leadership is absolutely critical in creating a climate in which such a change can take place, as Alan Hirsch and Tim Catchim pointedly write:

> *If we are not doing what a church should be doing*
> *then the task of leaders is to direct it to be the church*

*that it should be. And if leadership is unwilling to do this, then we suggest that they are abdicating their calling before God.*[25]

**FURTHER READING AND RESOURCES**

Steve Addison, *What Jesus Started*, Downers Grove, IL: IVP, 2012

Rodney Clapp, *A Peculiar People*, Downers Grove, IL: IVP, 1996

Erwin McManus, *An Unstoppable Force*, Orange, CA: Group, 2001

David Watson, *I Believe in the Church*, London: Hodder & Stoughton, 1978

Christian Schwarz, *Natural Church Development Handbook*, BCGA, 1996

The Natural Church Development Movement, based around the seminal work of Christian Schwarz, offer a variety of superb training resources including some extremely helpful surveys and other diagnostic tools designed to help local churches assess their own areas of strength and weakness. These can be found at http://training.ncd-uk.com/

# Suggested Itinerary For Church Leaders Awayday

One of the best ways of beginning the change process in a local church is to take the positional leaders away for a day conference. Getting out of our usual environment tends to facilitate less constrained ways of thinking. The day might be structured as follows:

1. Opening prayer and worship

2. Introductory teaching around some of the biblical understandings of the nature and calling of the church (bringing in an outside speaker/facilitator is often helpful). This could take the form of:

- *an exploration of some of the key hallmarks of the early church as described in the opening chapters of the Acts of the Apostles;*

- *an examination of some of the key biblical motifs used to describe the church;*

- *(in the absence of a speaker) as above, but with different groups either studying the different Bible passages that describe the calling of the church, or reflecting together on chapter 1 of this book.*

3. Each person is given a list of core characteristics of a healthy church (based on the input already given in the previous session) and invited to score our church from 0–5 on each characteristic. These characteristics might include:

- *welcoming to the outsider*

- *clear sense of calling and purpose*

- *engaged with the local community*

- *equipping every member for mission and ministry*

- *inspiring worship services in which the presence of God is sensed*

- *teaching which is inspiring and upbuilding for faith and life*

- *loving relationships*

- *openness to the promptings of the Spirit*

- *concern to imitate the works of Jesus*

- *generosity of heart*

- *concern for the least and the lost*

- *taking initiatives to make the Christian good news known to others*

4. Each person joins with one other peerson and each shares the three areas of greatest strength (the ones you have scored highest) and the three areas of most notable weakness. Discuss your reflections and reasons for scoring in this way with one another and then agree together which two areas you feel are the areas of greatest strength and which two are the areas of greatest weakness. This process should take around 20 minutes.

5. Each pair now joins with another pair and repeats the previous exercise, but this time offering to the other pair the two strengths and weaknesses they have jointly agreed upon. The four now agree together upon two principal areas of strength and two of weakness.

6. Each group of four now feed back their reflections to the wider group and results are noted by the facilitator.

7. Break for lunch and informal discussion.

8. Mix people up into groups of 4–6. Ask them to reflect on two questions (allocating 40 minutes for the first and 20 for the second):

- *What steps might we take in order to grow in the areas in which we feel ourselves to be weak as a church?*

- *What might we do in order to build on our areas of strength and to maximize such strengths?*

9. Give time for feedback and the compiling of suggestions for action.

10. Agree a process going forward in which a comprehensive action plan can be formulated and in which discussions can be taken further.

11. Closing prayer.

# 2

## Moving Things Forward:
## Leadership As A Catalyst For Change

What flourishing churches have in common is that they are led by people who possess and deploy the spiritual gift of leadership.[1]

In short, leadership is a complex phenomenon that touches on many other important organisational, social and personal processes. It depends on a process of influence, whereby people are inspired to work towards group goals, not through coercion, but through personal motivation.[2]

Leaders are not above others as much as ahead of others... discerning needs to be met, experimenting with new methods and approaches to familiar challenges... creating innovative structures, or finding new ways forward.[3]

Stephen Spielberg and Tom Hanks' brilliant TV mini-series *Band of Brothers* is the stirring account of the career of Easy Company of the US 506th Parachute Infantry Regiment throughout the final years of World War Two. The series has a particular poignancy in that its script and characterization are based around the real-life reminiscences of actual members of the company. These were the first men to land in occupied France in the early hours of 6 June 1944, charged with the task of preparing the way for the D-Day landings. In the face of significant challenges they disarmed German artillery, enabling Allied troops to move off the Normandy beaches. They heroically held the line against overwhelming odds and despite taking significant casualties at the height of the Battle of the Bulge, the final German counter-offensive before the end of the war. This was the company which captured Hitler's mountain retreat in the SS stronghold of Berchtesgaden.

The accomplishments of the men of Easy Company in those intense few months were staggering. Yet it could all have been so different. On the eve of going to war, morale in the company was at rock bottom, NCOs were threatening to resign and, although well trained physically, many among the ranks feared that they would be annihilated in combat. The reason? A completely ineffectual company commanding officer. Although he excelled at drilling troops on the parade ground, this was an officer with no ability to manage others, with a woeful lack of tactical combat acumen, and a profound insecurity in the face of more accomplished and more popular subordinate officers. Had Captain Herbert Sobell remained in charge, then it seems unlikely that Easy Company would ever have accomplished anything worthy of recording in a TV docudrama, even if sufficient members of the company had survived to record their reminiscences!

Providentially, from the first day of the European campaign, leadership of Easy Company fell to an exceptional young officer. Lieutenant Dick Winters blended tactical insight with exceptional relational and person-management skills, leading always by example. Without any concern for his own well-being or the advancement of his reputation, Winters took exactly the same bunch of dispirited men and inspired them to undreamed of heights in terms of performance and courage. The series, if nothing else, is a profound lesson in the vital importance of competent leadership and its impact for good or bad.

There is a growing realization in many spheres of life – whether that of business, politics, sport, or social enterprise – of the critical role leadership has to play in terms of the effectiveness and success of that enterprise. It's the reason why poor financial results inevitably lead to companies wanting to change their CEO or why underachieving football clubs believe that all their problems will be solved simply by changing the manager. It's why entire forests have been felled in order to produce the tsunami of leadership literature published in recent years,[4] and why a Google search around the word "leadership" flags up more than 200,000,000 articles and videos!

Richard Bolden writes of this phenomenon:

> *Leadership has become perhaps the most talked about issue in business and organisation – heralded as both the cause of and solution to most of the problems facing contemporary society. It is hard to turn on the television, open a newspaper, or attend an event without coming across numerous references to leaders, leadership, and leading.[5]*

This contemporary fascination with leadership may well be a reflection of a growing loss of fundamental purpose in society at large and in the lives of its members and a sense of being at the mercy of increasingly complex forces beyond our control. It may well reflect a longing for there to be a collection of people possessing some capacity to sort things out for us. Cynics might suggest that it arises from an instinct to avoid personal responsibility by pushing that responsibility onto some other "expert" figure, and from a desire to then have somebody to blame when things go wrong! However, history reveals to us that leadership, far from being a recently discovered phenomenon, is a quality that is sought after and necessary at all times and especially so in times of crisis and uncertainty, or at times of great change or transition.

So, it should hardly surprise us that the 2014 Church of England report *From Anecdote to Evidence,* based on extensive research into factors which generally affect church growth and decline, highlights effective leadership (defined as leadership which has the capacity to envision and motivate others and to lead innovation) as one of the most critical factors for healthy churches:

> *When asked about strengths in motivating people,*
> *more than three quarters of clergy who say they*
> *are better than most people at motivating people,*
> *inspiring and generating enthusiasm to action, lead*
> *growing churches. Among those who admit to being*
> *less able in this respect, growth is reported by just*
> *over a third.*[6]

When we turn to the Bible we find ample evidence to illustrate the vital importance of effective leadership. Although God is clearly identified as the unique leader of His people, it is equally clear that God chooses to exercise that leadership through faithful individuals and communities. When taking fresh initiatives with His people, or when seeking to call them back to Himself, or when responding to critical situations or threats in the life of His people, God's strategy is to raise up a leader, or a leadership group, through whom His plans might be brought to fruition.

There is little doubt that the people of Israel were perfectly aware of what God wanted of them in the years following their return to Jerusalem from exile in Babylon. They were not short of information. However, the force of their circumstances, the pressure of opposition from surrounding people groups, and the inertia which comes from becoming used to disappointment and discouragement all served to rob them of any will to rebuild their ruined city and get on with the task of fulfilling their calling to be a light to other nations. It required the arrival of Nehemiah, a leader called and envisioned by God, to get the stalled work of rebuilding back on track.

Given His long and consistent track record of acting in such a way, it should not surprise us that still today God's way of exercising influence is through raising up godly leadership. If we are to see local churches brought to fresh health and vitality and reinvigorated by a fresh understanding of their place in God's purposes, then the number one priority has to be the release of appropriate leadership. George Barna puts it pretty starkly:

> *After fifteen years of diligent digging into the world around me, I have reached the conclusion that the American church is dying due to a lack of strong leadership. In this time of unprecedented opportunity and plentiful resources, the church is actually losing influence. The primary reason is the lack of leadership. Nothing is more important than leadership.*[7]

What might such leadership look like, and how might it best be nurtured and developed?

## DEFINING LEADERSHIP

I am aware that, at this point, some readers may well be already on the verge of flicking on to the next chapter because they have never seen themselves as leaders and assume that all this leadership talk simply doesn't apply to them. May I ask you to stay with me a little longer? I hope to show that leadership might just have a broader compass; it might be a little more complex than some of us have realized and, truth be told, all of us can play a part in the practice of leadership. I have long felt that the most succinct summary of the true nature of the leadership task is that of John Maxwell, who suggests that "leadership is influence, nothing more, nothing less". Walter Wright develops this notion a little further:

> *If by leader we mean someone who holds a position of authority and responsibility, then every Christian is not a leader. But if by leader we mean a person who enters into relationship with another person to influence their behaviour, values or attitudes, then I would suggest that all Christians should be leaders. Or, perhaps, more accurately, all Christians should exercise leadership.*[8]

When it comes to the business of seeing kingdom vision and values becoming central to the life of our churches, then all of us have the capacity to play a part. All of us can exercise influence for God. It is likely that we can think of others who have exercised significant influence for good upon us at different stages in our spiritual growth and development. The likelihood is that many of them would not have fitted into many of the popular understandings of what a leader looks like.

Exercising leadership may be as simple as helping people to grow in their walk with God in exactly the same way as we ourselves have been helped by others. When we pare leadership down to this simple enterprise of exercising influence, it becomes something that now appears far more accessible to many more of us. The scope of our influence may well be different from that of others, but the reality is that if I am influencing others then I am exercising leadership. What often holds us back in exercising such leadership is the mistaken belief that only those who have either a leadership position or a natural talent for leadership are somehow qualified or entitled to lead. Let's dismantle those myths before we go further.

## Leadership is not just a position we hold

Some people, especially older generations, assume that the beginning and end of leadership consists in holding office or having a position. It is certainly the case, especially in some workplace contexts, that position usually confers a degree of authority upon those who hold it, and that such authority enables its holder to get others to follow their instructions, at least to some extent. However, there is no necessary overlap between position and leadership, and holding position by no means automatically implies having a clear calling to or suitability for that role. Indeed, sometimes people gravitate towards leadership positions only through a desire to be in the seat of power and to make sure that their voice is heard rather than through having some recognized leadership ability or experience. Some long for position because they feel it might fulfil some inner need for identity or significance. Others find themselves occupying formal roles because no one else will, and there is responsibility to be undertaken.

Position in and of itself does not, of course, convey any ability to fulfil any role. This means that leadership which is purely based on holding position rests on a weak foundation and will never be very effective. People will only follow a positional leader within the bounds of their stated authority and then often only grudgingly. Positional leadership alone is rarely, if ever, inspirational and thus never really has the capacity to motivate people or to move things forward. Although most local churches have people occupying "leadership" positions, many fail to grow or to progress because that positional leadership, whether lay or ordained, is poor and unimaginative. As a contemporary writer observes:

> *Many leaders have no vision of what God wishes to birth through the congregation because they spend all their time and energy nursing things that want to die. A strong reason for continued atrophy in many congregations is that vital resources and energies continue to be spent on maintaining life-support systems for comatose programmes, agencies, markets and rituals.*[9]

It is striking that most of those who stand out as significant leaders among the biblical narratives do not do so by virtue of having any formal leadership position. Moses had spent decades in the wilderness as a herdsman, reflecting on the life he could have had and the consequences of his earlier life choices. God used him to lead the downtrodden Hebrew slaves out of the clutches of the most powerful empire of the day and then to form them painstakingly into a people fit for God's purposes.[10]

Gideon, a fearful little man whom we meet in a winepress, threshing grain, describes himself as the youngest member of the least family in an insignificant tribe – not an obvious qualification for any leadership position. Everyone was ahead of him in the pecking order, yet he was the man whom God used to deliver the oppressed Israelites from Midianite subjugation.[11]

David, the king under whom Israel became a mighty nation and began to fulfil its destiny as God's special people, and perhaps the most significant of all Old Testament leaders, spent his early career as a fugitive from his tyrannical predecessor, Saul. Far from having any recognized position, David was effectively an outlaw, yet his leadership outstripped that of the positional leader, Saul, in every way.[12]

As we have observed, Nehemiah is the archetypal reengineering leader whose achievements were monumental. Yet, although he held position in the court of the Persian emperor, there is no suggestion that this gave him any direct authority over the affairs of Jerusalem, the theatre of his subsequent operations. The book that describes his exploits does list a number of positional leaders, both religious and political.[13] These are exactly those who have failed, thus far, to put into action God's intentions. Nehemiah has no position as such, but is merely someone who "had come to seek the welfare of the sons of Israel".[14]

Ideally, leadership positions should be filled by those who have leadership qualities and supremely those who are recognized as having the ability to influence others positively. But position doesn't make you into a leader, and lack of position by no means excludes you from exercising leadership.

## Leadership is not necessarily a talent with which we were born

Up until the late twentieth century there existed a reasonably widespread assumption that leaders are heroic figures who are made of different stuff from the rest of us. Originating with what has been termed "The Great Man" doctrine of leadership, fuelled by blockbuster Hollywood movies, and perpetuated by mid-twentieth century business leadership models, leadership has been seen as a trait that some possess and others don't. It is probably this, somewhat incomplete, thinking that is most responsible for making many of us feel that we could never be leaders.

It is certainly true that some people seem to be "born" leaders. In whatever situation they find themselves they always seem to end up leading. However, the fact that some apparently possess innate leadership traits does not mean that all others are excluded from the ranks of leadership. Warren Bennis and Burt Nanus insist that:

> *Whatever natural endowments we bring to the role of leadership, they can be enhanced; nurture is far more important than nature in determining who becomes a successful leader.*[15]

Some biblical characters do seem to be the kind of people who would be recognized as demonstrating leadership traits from an early age. Joseph was certainly not backwards in coming forward in his early years, and one suspects that the apostle Peter would have been at the forefront in any situation in which he found himself. Yet both had to undergo significant personal formation — much of which came about through some painful experiences — before they were in a position whereby they could exercise positive leadership influence. Natural giftedness by itself is rarely sufficient for effective leadership, and there is no guarantee that "born" leaders will lead well.

Yet many of those who emerge in the Scriptures as significant leaders are far from being recognized as natural leaders. Timothy has to be continually reminded by his mentor, the apostle Paul, to withstand his own natural fear and reserve and instead to be strong in the power of God's indwelling Spirit. Nehemiah's leadership capacity seems to have been a product of his passionate concern for the restoration of God's kingdom on earth rather than any innate ability. It was nurtured as he prayed and fasted and offered himself to God for the task of rebuilding the ruined city.

So what encouragement might there be for those of us who do not have leadership position (or at least, not position that gives us great influence), or who do not see ourselves as especially gifted, natural leaders, and yet who have a deep longing to see our churches renewed, our communities transformed, and the influence of God's kingdom growing? The implication from Scripture seems to be this: those who cultivate hearts that are captivated by God's purposes, allowing themselves to be shaped by encounter with Him, may well be those who find themselves exercising influence in and for God's kingdom. This need not be in the capacity of a formal leadership position. All of us can grow in our effectiveness if we apply ourselves to learning and honing those skills and disciplines that will enable us to lead well in the specific places to which God calls us. Bennis and Nanus underline this truth with their reminder that:

> *Leadership seems to be the marshalling of skills possessed by a majority but used by a minority. But it is something which can be learned by anyone, taught to everyone, denied to no-one.*[16]

So what precisely are these attributes and disciplines that form the basis of kingdom leadership? As we reflect on the kind of leadership which is required today in order that our churches might be fit for purpose, we are going to look a little more closely at the characteristics of Nehemiah's leadership in the hope of learning some lessons from a master rebuilder.

## THE HALLMARKS/CHARACTERISTICS OF EFFECTIVE LEADERSHIP

### 1. Passion

It is easy to assume that those who achieve much as leaders are just exceptionally gifted or talented people, or that the context in which they work is somehow easier than others (and certainly than the place in which I work!). My own experience of such leaders is not that they have necessarily greater gifts than others, but rather greater passion and more deeply held convictions. This was certainly the root of Nehemiah's extraordinary effectiveness. Here is a man who is absorbed with God and with a desire to see His Kingdom grow and His name honoured. His delight, he tells us, is in belonging to God and in worshipping and revering God's name[17] because of the great things God has done in saving his people. He has immersed himself so thoroughly in the Scriptures that his whole thinking, attitudes, and expectations are now profoundly shaped by the will and purposes of God. Whatever Nehemiah's outward gifts and qualities, all of them flow out of a rich inner life that is deeply rooted in a familiarity with the presence of God and a corresponding longing to serve and please Him.

The clear relationship between passion for God and effectiveness shouldn't surprise us when we reflect again on our basic understanding of leadership as *influence*. Those who are shaped by a deep relationship with God become attractive and winsome people. Their closeness to God gives them influence and authority; others long to experience what they have experienced and are keen to be led by them. Without spiritual passion, positional leadership is sterile and impotent. If the *natural* or *born* leader lacks rootedness in God, he or she will become an unreliable leader, influencing people along ways which may not be in line with those of God and His kingdom.

When trying to identify emerging leaders in my own church, I have always looked first for those who display spiritual passion and a growing love for God. My conviction is that if this foundation is in place, then God is well able to add whatever else is required in order to grow such people as effective leaders. My observation is that such people are precisely those whom God most often calls and prompts to seize opportunities for growing His kingdom. What is more, when the going gets tough and we are faced with significant leadership challenges, probably the only thing that will have the capacity to keep us going is the strength of conviction which comes from having a deeply rooted connection with God.

This is why one of the top priorities for any effective leader is to make sure that we pay the closest attention to growing in our walk with God. Like Nehemiah this will mean immersing ourselves in God's word. It will mean seeking His presence. It will be fostered by fasting and praying as a way of resisting temptations that might distract us. It will mean seeking to grow in our concern for the things that are closest to God's heart. Passion produces energy, the kind of energy which uniquely has the capacity to engineer movement and change.

## 2. Transformation

Authentic leadership will always have a focus on moving things forward and is thus principally concerned with enabling change to come about. As Peter Senge puts it:

> *Leadership is always in a sense about change. Leaders work to bring about a different order of things. Their focus is invariably on the new, on what is trying to emerge.*[18]

If this is true about leadership generally it is doubly true about leadership in the kingdom of God. Although there will always be core components common to any expression of leadership, the specific nature and purpose of any enterprise will have a profound bearing on what forms and styles of leadership may or may not be appropriate in that enterprise. When we examine the motifs used to define God's kingdom throughout the Bible we find that there is something fundamentally dynamic and transformational to them, and that such an outlook shapes the nature of kingdom leadership.

Many of Jesus' metaphors for the kingdom are ones of growth and change, and raise an expectation in us that kingdom ministry will always, in some way, involve growth, transformation, and development. God is described as a God who is forever making all things new. His kingdom is like a mustard seed which, although very tiny, produces a plant that is so invasive it takes over the whole plot.[19] It is like a seed that grows of its own accord,[20] or like leaven which permeates the whole lump of dough,[21] causing it to rise. The Christian gospel is one that has at its core the transformation and renewal of people.[22] The church is an entity which grows in size and influence and which has a mandate to advance to the very ends of the earth.[23]

The entire mood of the New Testament is eschatological; life is lived against the backdrop of an expectation that history is moving to a climax in which Jesus, having inaugurated His kingdom on earth during His earthly ministry, will return to consummate that kingdom and to bring about the renewal of all things.[24] Leaders who emerge from such an entity and who carry genuine kingdom DNA will always be involved in the business of moving things forward and of facilitating growth. They will embody a godly restlessness, an appropriate sense of dissatisfaction with the status quo.

Of course the leadership that we see in the life of the first Christian communities was profoundly forward-looking and focused on bringing transformation and change. The thrust of the preaching of Peter and Stephen in the early chapters of the Acts of the Apostles is that the life and ministry of Jesus has ushered in a whole new era in God's dealings with humankind and has rendered obsolete the practices and assumptions of the previous age. Thus, the only appropriate response to this event is that of *repentance*, a change of attitude and outlook. Life must now be lived from a completely changed perspective. It is these same convictions which impel the church in Antioch to commission Barnabas and Saul for the groundbreaking work of planting new churches and of helping others discover the transforming power of the gospel in their own lives.

The apostle Paul describes leadership and ministry[25] as being fivefold in nature. An examination of the church in recent years might lead to the assumption that, of all the five forms of leadership referenced in Ephesians 4, those of "pastor" and "teacher" (the two less obviously focused on pioneering as opposed to maintaining) are clearly the most important. However, as Hirsch and Catchim point out,[26] the word "pastor" has no other mention in the New Testament, while the word "teacher" occurs only ten times. When we analyse the New Testament documents we find that the particular ministry role that is to the forefront and that is most often mentioned is that of "apostle". The ministry and leadership functions of the church are, in fact, intended to be primarily focused on breaking new ground for the kingdom.

If this is generally true of kingdom leaders it is especially true of those who find themselves in contexts in which God's work has apparently stalled. Nehemiah's passion for God found very practical expression in a longing to see God's city rebuilt[27] and a clear and strategic intention to do whatever he could in order to be a catalyst for such a change to come about in the city's fortunes. His resolution to see this change come about was rooted in a conviction that this was not an exceptional or unusual task to be accomplished, but rather exactly what might be considered normal for those who belong to a God who is *forever making all things new.*[28]

One of the reasons so many churches remain stuck in decline is that they are led by those who do not have a growth mindset or who see their own role as rather more passive. The *From Anecdote to Evidence* research quoted earlier noted that where clergy adopted more static, empathetic, and managerial styles of ministry, church decline was much more likely.[29] The specific context in which leadership is exercised will always have a bearing on what that leadership should look like. Leadership in a jazz ensemble, which has been playing together for many years, and which has an established sense of common purpose and direction, will look different to that in a newly formed dance company meeting to rehearse for the very first time. For either to appropriate the style of the other would lead to sterility for the one and inertia for the other, and in each case a frustration of purpose.

The mistake that many positional church leaders make is of not understanding or embracing a style of leadership that is most suitable for a context in which the only options are either radical change or entropy. They may be fearful of provoking conflict or simply feel ill equipped to embrace a more proactive leadership style. As a result, many resort to a more democratic approach (which in this context may well really be an abdication of leadership) in the hope that somehow, one day, everyone will come to the same conclusion about the need for change and magically embrace it. It rarely, if ever, happens.

If we are to see widespread change in the face of established churches then we need leaders who are prepared to lead and who are prepared to embrace a calling to a ministry that will have at least something of an apostolic flavour to it. Such leaders will need to recognize that their call from God involves fostering godly dissatisfaction and unease with the way things are, and being effective catalysts for kingdom change. It will be such leaders who inspire their congregations to see different ways of doing things, and energize people to see those changes come to pass, even in the face of uncertainty.

## 3. Relationship

Notions of leadership as being the sole province of the "Heroic Leader", who is "Large and in Charge" and who rides into town in order to right all wrongs and to turn everything around, may have been fashionable and attractive in previous ages but may not be the most helpful models for us today. As will become obvious throughout this book, I am firmly convinced of the importance of the role of visionary leaders and long to see more and more raised up. However, I am distressed when I see churches damaged through the impact of insensitive leadership that seeks to impose its will and vision in a somewhat unilateral manner, paying little attention to the consequences for those on the receiving end, and justifying this on the basis of some leadership principle.

Such dissonant styles of leadership rarely if ever achieve anything worthwhile and usually breed pain and distress, discontent, and resentment. Far from advancing the work of the kingdom they tend to set it back, often by many years. Fundamental to effective leadership is the realization that leadership, because it is basically to do with people, is a relational enterprise,[30] an active partnership between leaders and followers. As Walter Wright puts it:

> *Leadership is a relationship between two persons in which one person seeks to influence the behaviour, attitudes, values or vision of another. It is always a relationship and it always rests in the hands of the followers. It does not matter what our title is or how*

*much authority we think we have. Unless someone chooses to follow, we have not led. Leadership finds its expression in relationships.*[31]

It goes without saying that such relationships can never be manipulative ones but rather are founded on a commitment to bringing the best for and out of followers. We will explore later some specific strategies for building the leadership relationship and for getting followers on board, but suffice for now to say that the only effective leadership is that which takes seriously the reality of its relational nature.[32]

Early on in my career as a League cricketer, I played under one of the worst team captains I have ever come across. The role of captain in a cricket team is vitally important. Not only is he continually having to make key tactical decisions which will significantly affect the outcome of the match, but he is also responsible for bringing the best out of the players he has, taking ten other individuals and forming them into a team. This particular captain was an able cricketer, but hopeless at managing others. Mistakes in the field were greeted with impatience, and a culture of fear permeated the team. Although the team contained a number of highly gifted players, it consistently underperformed and few actually enjoyed playing.

The last captain under whom I played was the exact opposite. Tactically shrewd but also hugely encouraging of others, even when they made mistakes, he managed to create a team environment in which everyone strove to give of their best. Although the talent pool available to him was not exceptional, he formed the individual players into an effective team which consistently achieved results way in excess of expectations. Most significantly, this captain, through a strongly relational leadership style, led a team in which everyone appreciated that they had a key role to play, that the performance of the team mattered far more than that of any individual player, and in which everyone was motivated to try their hardest for a captain to whom they felt personally connected.

Nehemiah's way of operating shows him to be a leader who clearly understands the strongly relational nature of effective leadership. In his first recorded conversation with the inhabitants of Jerusalem there is a profound identification with the people. "You see the bad situation *we* are in," he begins. "Come, let *us* rebuild the wall of Jerusalem so that *we* will no longer be a reproach."[33] These are not empty words. As the narrative unfolds, it becomes apparent[34] that Nehemiah is thoroughly involved in the practical work of rebuilding, taking his own share of the heavy work alongside everyone else. Furthermore, although he has now been appointed governor of Jerusalem, he refuses to benefit from the allowances and privileges which would be his by virtue of his office,[35] preferring to put aside those things which might distance him or set him apart from his co-labourers.

Relational leaders are not only those who demonstrate themselves to be invested in the things that matter to those people whom they are called to lead and who identify themselves as one among those people; they are also leaders who realize that we can only influence those whose trust and confidence we have somehow won. For this to take place, relationships need to be built.

## 4. Focus

As a child growing up my favourite TV programme was broadcast on Friday teatime. From getting out of school mid-afternoon my sense of anticipation and excitement grew until five o' clock arrived and *Crackerjack* came on the box. A fast-moving (for the sixties, at least!) mix of comedy, music, and team games, the climax to each week's show was the *Crackerjack* quiz, in which four contestants were each asked questions in turn. Correct answers meant that you were given a prize to hold; incorrect answers resulted in your being given a large paper "cabbage". After each round the number of things you were holding grew in number. The first person to drop anything from their arms, whether prize or booby prize, was eliminated, and the last person standing was the overall winner. The more bulky cabbages you were trying to hold onto, the greater chance you had of elimination.

My childhood dream was to take part in that game. As a church leader, I feel I have been playing it most of my life! For most of us, the number of things we are invited (or expected) to hold far exceed our capacity to do so. The challenge is to refuse to take on the "cabbages" in order to make sure that we don't drop the really valuable things, and this, of course, implies being able to recognize what is, and what is not, a cabbage. The only way we can succeed in determining what our priorities should be is to have absolute clarity about our specific calling. For those involved in leading change in local churches, the one thing that will prevent us from fulfilling this calling is to succumb to the pressure (whether from ourselves or from others) to maintain every activity currently taking place and every responsibility traditionally undertaken by the minister, as well as making time for leading the change we are seeking to bring about. Norman Shawchuck and Roger Heuser suggest that:

> *Many congregations talk of wanting a leader but exert great pressure to make the pastor into a manager, because managers can be domesticated, but leaders have a vision and passion that cannot be fully tamed.*[36]

Not only do we not have time to do everything, but we also don't have the emotional energy or the headspace. I have found it helpful at different times to agree an informal "contract" with other responsible officers in the church. In this we agree together what should be the priorities, in terms of my allocation of time and energies, given my calling and commitment and responsibility of moving the church forward. I have made it clear that I cannot take on other significant areas of responsibility without giving up existing ones, and have, at times, invited suggestions as to what the PCC[37] would like me to stop doing if they thought that I ought to take on, or take back, other responsibilities.

Settling in your own mind a simple list of key priorities in advance (you could make it the subject of a Retreat Day and discuss it with the Lord) will help you to make decisions as to whether or not to take on specific responsibilities when they arise. Do they help you achieve your stated objectives, or do they get in the way? Providing "services" for spiritual consumers has always seemed to me a poor and unfaithful use of my time. Developing people in such a way that they grow in their capacity to exercise influence for the kingdom has always seemed to be exactly what I ought to be doing. So, one question I will always ask of some activity or opportunity which presents itself is "Will this grow kingdom capacity in people?" I am also clear that I need to guard time for strategic praying, thinking, and planning and thus must make sure that I do not allow my diary to become so full, even with worthwhile things, that such time is squeezed out.

One of the qualities I admire most in Nehemiah is his clear sense of focus and his refusal to be knocked off course or deflected from his understood priorities. When his enemies sow fear into the hearts of the Jewish people Nehemiah reassures them and keeps them focused by reminding them of God's character and power and that their task is in response to His call.[38] When he faces personal threats and when his enemies try to entice him away from the work in order to meet with them (and presumably guarantee his own safety), Nehemiah's consistent response is that he is engaged in a great work and cannot leave it for any lesser purpose.[39]

We may not be likely to face threats to our lives as a result of sticking our necks out for the kingdom; however, we may lose favour with those who are threatened by what we are seeking to do, and may even lose our reputation because of the criticism of others. One of the things that always has the capacity to distract us and to absorb time and energy unnecessarily is the desire to justify ourselves. Nehemiah understands that the best way of vindicating himself is simply to press on with the work and to see it come to fruition. Even when the wall is completely rebuilt, Nehemiah's focus does not slip. He understands that his calling is not simply to bring about physical, but also moral and spiritual, restoration to the city. He now begins to apply himself[40] to helping the people reorder their lives according to the requirements of God's neglected Law.

As well as maintaining personal focus, Nehemiah gloriously fulfils the calling of the effective leader to take primary responsibility for ensuring that the whole church is reminded of its calling and purpose. As Stephen Cottrell puts it:

> *The most important quality in terms of day to day leadership is the willingness to recall the organisation to its primary vocation... The leader is the one who dares the whole organisation to stop for a minute and take time out to remember why they are there.*[41]

## 5. Humility

True humility comes from understanding that our leadership is, when all is said and done, delegated responsibility, a spiritual gift from God for the exercise of which we are wholly dependent upon Him. Nehemiah has no doubt that his leadership has only arisen because of God's favour and that the success of his project is dependent entirely upon Him.[42] At every step of the way, and especially when faced with challenges, it is to God whom Nehemiah turns for help.[43] His refusal of the privileges of position is of a piece with his sense of being accountable to God and of the need to walk humbly before his God.

Such leaders are winsome leaders. They are exactly the people whom we feel we might trust and who will lead us responsibly and well. What is more, these are leaders who stand the best chance of being in it for the long haul and of staying emotionally and spiritually healthy. Because they understand that God is the one who carries ultimate responsibility, they do not take upon themselves an inappropriate sense of responsibility for the success or failure of their enterprise. Their own sense of self-worth and significance is not ultimately tied up in their role. They are simply thrilled to be entrusted with the privilege of serving and of working together with God for the advance of His kingdom.

These are the kind of leaders whom God is looking to raise up and to release in order that more and more local churches might truly be fit for and restored to their original purpose. In the following chapters we are going to examine some of the specific practices and disciplines such leaders will need to develop in order to be truly effective in the fulfilment of their calling.

## FURTHER READING AND RESOURCES

Warren Bennis and Burt Nanus, *Leaders*, New York: Harper Collins, 2007

Ajith Fernando, *Jesus Driven Ministry*, Leicester: IVP, 2002

Alan Hirsch and Tim Catchim, *The Permanent Revolution*, San Francisco, CA: Jossey-Bass, 2012

Bill Hybels, *Courageous Leadership*, Grand Rapids, MI: Zondervan, 2002.

James Lawrence, *Growing Leaders*, Oxford: BRF, 2004.

Alan Roxburgh and Fred Romanuk, *The Missional Leader*, San Francisco, CA: Jossey-Bass, 2006.

The Church Pastoral Aid Society (CPAS) have developed a range of extremely helpful materials for use in local churches designed to promote the development of leaders. Foremost among these is their excellent *Growing Leaders* course. Full details of this, and other related materials, can be found on their website: http://www.cpas.org.uk/church-resources/growing-leaders-suite/growing-leaders

# 3

## Imagining The Future: Articulating Vision That Stirs The Heart

I believe that creating a vision is the most important function of leadership. A good vision establishes a beacon of light that both the leader and the followers can latch onto and use to guide them from the day to day minutiae that can potentially sidetrack even the most pure of heart. A vision is simply a picture of an ideal state of what the leader wants his or her organisation to be sometime in the future.[1]

Vision creates faith and inspires hope. Vision provides the energy for every effort, the power that will penetrate the problems and the will that overcomes obstacles. Vision is usually accompanied by a profound dissatisfaction with the way things are and a compelling perception of the way things could be. Vision starts with frustration over what is and develops with determination to press towards what could be. Vision orientates with the indignation of hindsight, the illumination of insight and the imagination of foresight.[2]

What a great visionary leader does is awaken and harness the dreams and visions of the members of a given community and give them deeper coherence by means of a grand vision that ties together all the little visions of the members of the group.[3]

had just led my first Sunday evening service as vicar of Emmanuel Church Saltburn, a service of Prayer Book Evensong, and I was standing at the back of church contemplating the size of the task facing me as I embarked upon what would inevitably be a lengthy journey of bringing about change. Common Prayer sung Evensong with an organ, and a robed choir which slightly outnumbered the rest of the congregation, hadn't seemed to me to be the most inspiring worship experience. Judging by the posture of the others attending, it didn't seem to provoke any great sense of anticipation of meeting with God, or any other grounds for excitement. As the congregation filed out and as I shook hands with people, an elderly man, who for some reason was visiting the church that evening, hesitated and then turned back to speak to me. "Do you believe that God speaks to us sometimes through pictures and visions?" he asked me. When I informed him that I certainly did he went on to explain that as he had been sitting in church that evening, he had seen, in the Spirit, a river flowing down through the middle of the church building, and people coming from all around the surrounding area to drink. Then he walked away, and I never saw him again.

It was a wonderful token of God's grace for us, and a remarkable encouragement as we settled into our task of turning around a local church. Like most prophetic words or pictures, it didn't convey something completely out of the blue, but rather reinforced and underlined a sense of what God had already been speaking to us. It was as if God were saying, this really is my vision for my church and I am just as committed to seeing it come about here as anywhere else.

Within the space of a few years Emmanuel Saltburn had become not just a place where members of the local community were discovering new life in Christ and experiencing "times of refreshing" from the Lord,[4] but also something of a place of resourcing, equipping, and encouragement for people from other local churches. Indeed, less than three years after that evening, when the PCC spent some time engaging in a process of discerning and drafting a vision statement for our church, they ended up with one that perfectly reflected this prophetic picture: "To grow in the love of Christ, and to share it with others". In the more challenging times that lay ahead, among other things, it was the vision encapsulated in this prophetic picture that kept me going.

Leaders are catalysts for change. One of their prime responsibilities is to help others embrace God's preferred future for their church or other organization and buy into it. For a number of reasons this is not necessarily a straightforward task. It may be that leaders move into situations where the church whose oversight they inherit are longing for change and fresh direction (this was the case with my current church when I arrived). It is far more likely, however, that any significant change is perceived as threatening, and that the bulk of people concerned have a determination to keep things, as far as possible, just as they are. The status quo (which one wit has described as Latin for "the mess we are in"!) is at least familiar, and gives us a sense of certainty and security.

A desire to preserve it may be due to all manner of reasons. People of a certain age, who may be experiencing threatening changes in life for the first time (such as children moving away from home, the loss or decline of elderly parents, personal health issues, possible unemployment), have a vested interest in one aspect of life, at least, remaining constant. Clinging on to forms of church life that represent a link with a diminishing but precious past is often a reaction to change overload. For others, maintaining things as they have always been (at least in our living memory) may well be due to a misplaced sense of loyalty to forebears, to parents or grandparents who were instrumental in the founding of this church (a major issue for a Methodist church with which I once had some connection), or who held office in the church in the past or shaped it in other ways. Sometimes it is a fear of losing what we have and a lack of certainty in terms of what we might gain through any change. People have not yet been persuaded that there might exist a preferable future with benefits that outweigh anything we are currently experiencing.

Sometimes it is not opposition that is the biggest threat to impetus for change, but inertia born out of a sense of hopelessness or disappointment. The experience of decline over a number of years – often compounded by the apparent failure of previous initiatives to halt or reverse such decline – leads to an inability, or at least an unwillingness, to think that anything positive might happen here ever again. Previous ministers may well have come and gone, none staying long enough to make a significant impact for good, and each, never deliberately, but implicitly, giving the impression that this was not a place worth investing in for the long haul. Saltburn had had seven different vicars in the forty-five years immediately prior to my arrival. It took us quite a while to convince people that, for us, this was not simply a stepping-stone to a more worthwhile or prestigious ministry, and that we were here until God called us away, and if necessary, for the rest of our lives.

When Nehemiah made the journey to Jerusalem in order to galvanize the people of Jerusalem into rebuilding their city walls, and thus to restore the honour of the living God among the nations, the primary issue with which he had to contend was disappointment and a crippling lack of hope. The walls of Jerusalem had been torn down over 100 years previously. People had simply got used to the ruins and had ceased to imagine that anything could be different.

When the first returning exiles had summoned the courage to try to make something out of the ruins and had begun to rebuild the walls and erect some new gates, the leaders of the local mixed race tribes had taken exception, seeing the resurrection of Jerusalem as a potential threat to their own interests and an opportunity to exercise influence. Making up some spurious reasons as to why the renewal of Jerusalem would not be in the interests of the Persian emperor, they wrote to the emperor insisting that he order the work to be halted.[5] When the emperor accedes to their requests, they take up arms against the inhabitants of Jerusalem, force them to stop their rebuilding work, and tear down the repaired walls and gates. Little wonder that there was such a reluctance to pick up tools again. The people had suffered the grievous blow of having hopes raised only to have them cruelly dashed once more. Moreover, the threats of their neighbours still rang loudly in their ears, and they had little incentive to provoke them again. All hope of a better future had completely evaporated.

Whatever the factors set against us (some will be obvious and even expressed openly, whil others will be more covert and not even necessarily understood by their proponents) and whatever the threats to movement and change, one thing is certain: we will never be able to overcome them simply by force of personality. Neither is it ever enough simply to insist that our way is better, or even that it is more in line with Scripture, or that it has anything else to commend it and thus trump any rival convictions. Something different is required. Leaders who are effective in bringing about change succeed because they have mastered a number of vital disciplines. Foremost among these is that of articulating and commending a vision of a preferable future in such a way that others share it and commit to it.

## THE VITAL IMPORTANCE OF VISION

Bill Hybels describes vision as "the leader's most potent weapon",[6] while Walter Wright[7] insists that "Articulating the vision may be the single most important responsibility that a leader has." What do we mean when we speak of casting or commending vision?

Vision-casting is essentially the ability to see and understand the preferred future which we believe God intends for us. It involves communicating effectively a description and understanding of this to others in such a way that they own it and become motivated to invest their own efforts and energies towards seeing it come about. Vision is a potent tool because it seems to be the one thing with the capacity to fire people's imaginations and stir their hearts in such a way that they become willing to leave behind the familiarity of the status quo and take the risk of embracing change. Visionary leaders have clarity when it comes to discerning the direction in which they believe they should lead the church, and also the capacity, over time, to bring a majority of the members of the church on board in pursuing such a direction rather than any other. No wonder that one writer is able to describe vision as "putting the match to the fuel that most people carry around in their hearts and long to have ignited", while Walter Wright observes:

> *Vision is seeing tomorrow so powerfully that it shapes today... The first responsibility of leadership is to articulate the vision, to keep the mission and values before the church or organisation. Effective leaders offer a compelling picture of the future that motivates people to get involved.*[8]

The key to Nehemiah's success in breaking through the inertia that prevailed in Jerusalem and in enabling progress with the work of rebuilding was his ability as a visionary leader. The turnaround in people's hopes and aspirations takes place as Nehemiah paints a picture for them of what might be, of how God appears already to be involved in facilitating their future, and of how the people themselves might play a part in seeing all this come to fruition.[9] This is a picture of a future that is not only more attractive than the current reality, but is, more importantly, seen to be realistic and attainable as opposed to being merely wishful thinking. It is the fact that it is both desirable and also within reach which produces passion and stimulates action. When we begin to analyse the specific ways in which such vision contributes to the momentum of a church or, for that matter, any other organization, we see that its impact is broad in scope.

## Generating hope

Most churches, even those that appear to be stuck in a form of self-serving traditionalism, have aspirations for a different and better future. Such aspirations may be little more than a vague hope that one day there might be more (and usually younger!) people joining the church. By and large the expectation is that this might come about through a change of heart in those who are not currently part of the church rather than any change in culture or practice on the part of the church itself! Aspirations are helpful, but do not in and of themselves generate any sense of movement, let alone a clear direction of travel for the church. This is why so many churches simply continue to do what they have always done albeit, perhaps, with fewer resources and on a reduced scale, and why at every level, from denominational to local, churches find themselves increasingly in the business of managing decline. What is required is fresh hope that things might be different. Vision is that which engenders such hope. It has this capacity because it flows out of an understanding of God's purposes for us and helps connect people afresh to those purposes. As Bennis and Nanus remind us: "A vision articulates a view of a realistic, credible, attractive future for the organisation, a condition that is better in some important ways than what now exists."[10]

Visionary leadership begins with the telling of God's story in such a way that people grow in their understanding that this is a story which is still unfolding as it moves towards its fulfilment in Jesus, and that all of us are actors who have a part to play today in God's unfolding purposes. When I can plot my own life against the backdrop of this story, then I encounter a hope which will motivate and sustain me. The role of the leader is to paint such a backdrop by telling that story.

## Setting direction

When I learned to drive, I found the business of steering a car somewhat challenging – distracted, perhaps, by all the other complicated processes such as balancing the different pedals. In my first couple driving lessons my instructor had to keep grabbing the wheel in order to correct my wayward steering. As I set off for my third lesson, I was determined to master this clearly rather difficult art. In order to keep a much closer watch on the car's direction, I fixed my eyes firmly on the front of the car bonnet. Once again I was all over the road! My instructor, with the kind of insight that probably qualifies people to be driving instructors, pointed out straight away what I was doing wrong, and told me to look away from the bonnet and to fix my eyes on the middle distance. This seemed to me to be a very dangerous suggestion. Goodness only knows where the car might end up if I took my eye off it! However, he was the driving instructor, so I thought I ought to humour him. Remarkably, when I did fix my attention on the road ahead, the car seemed to follow my eyes. I have never subsequently had any problems with steering!

The secret I learned about steering a car is equally applicable when it comes to giving direction to a church. The temptation is always to have our attention absorbed by whatever might be today's most pressing issue, to be reactive in terms of how we invest our time and other resources. To be free of this, we need to have a sense of where the road ahead might be taking us and then keep our eyes fixed upon that destination. Only then can we expect to make any progress. Bennis and Nanus describe vision as a target that beckons, while others have likened it to a compass that helps us set a direction. Shawchuck and Heuser describe it in these terms:

> *The congregation's corporate vision becomes a path where there is no pathway; it brings clarity when there is obscurity and provides the impetus to keep going no matter how formidable the roadblocks. Vision transcends; it lifts the entire congregation to new realisations of possibilities; it generates enthusiasm and power; it aligns the thoughts, emotions and actions of the people in pursuit of a common and compelling purpose.*[11]

Vision gives us something credible at which to aim and injects a sense of purpose into the very heart of a church. It keeps us from simply wandering aimlessly, or from leaping onto any and every latest bandwagon. This is why — if we want to help a church move beyond its current state into a more functional way of being — we will need to give people a compelling vision of a possible new future on which they can fix their eyes and hearts and which will help them navigate their way towards it. Many leaders with a strong aspiration to bring about change in the churches they lead experience great frustration because people seem unwilling to move with them in the way they are convinced God is leading. Usually this is because they have not spent enough time articulating vision in a way that makes it sufficiently clear for people to head towards.

## Creating ownership

Not only does vision serve to give focus to a congregation generally, but it also helps individuals recognize their own place in God's purposes for their church and helps people to "buy in" to the new journey on which the church is now travelling. Some have described vision as a magnet which draws people in and thus increases their sense of ownership of that journey. This is why, as we will explore more fully later, the casting of vision has to be done in such a way that it connects with and takes seriously the specific concerns and aspirations of those to whom we are seeking to commend that vision. As James Kouzes and Barry Posner point out:

> *Leaders... breathe life into visions. They communicate hopes and dreams so that others clearly understand and share them as their own. They show others how their values and interests will be served by the long-term vision of the future.*[12]

One of the striking things about Nehemiah's leadership in Jerusalem is the way in which he managed, apparently, to galvanize the entire community to engage in the work of rebuilding. Nehemiah 3 details the different aspects of the work undertaken by the different families, professions, and other groups of people, each focusing on their own specific area of responsibility but all inspired by a common vision of seeing the whole wall restored. A compelling vision not only aligns people with a shared purpose but also serves to release the resources that are essential to the accomplishment of that vision. As Shawchuck and Heuser observe:

> *The essence of leadership is the ability to influence others to volunteer their separate energies and resources to a common pursuit. This rests on the leader's ability to communicate the vision in a clear, convincing and compelling manner. The communication must excite not only people's intellects but also their imagination and passion.*[13]

One of the clearest indications to me, after three years in Saltburn, that we were heading in the right direction and getting buy-in was that financial giving to the church had doubled in that period. A church which had been rather over-dependent upon money-raising schemes to pay its way was now resourced by the direct giving of its members. As one wit rather pithily expressed it, "When the person with the vision meets the person with the money, the person with the money gets the vision, and the person with the vision gets the money!"

## Providing clarity

One of the most awkward moments I have ever witnessed in a local church was that of hearing a relatively newly installed vicar preaching to the fairly traditional congregation he was now overseeing. In his sermon he explained that what the congregation needed if it was to thrive was to change in some key ways, but that he, the vicar, was not clear as to what that change might look like. Not only did I wince inwardly, but I could almost sense the congregation stiffen as they positioned themselves to grip ever more tightly onto that which was familiar to them and as they steeled themselves to resist whatever it was that the vicar might try to foist upon them.

Few people find change palatable and many are downright terrified by the prospect of it. What is most disturbing about change is the uncertainty that it brings. The effective management of change is all about allaying such fears and dispelling as much uncertainty as possible. At the heart of vision-casting is the painting of pictures of the future which generate confidence. Vision is all about giving definition to the direction of travel. It is as much about helping people understand what we will *not* be doing and where we will *not* be going as it is about setting out a path along which we are going to travel.

Vision sets parameters to the change and transition we are going to undertake. Change becomes not something to be feared, and certainly not something which is open-ended and indeterminate. Rather, it becomes something which is defined and restricted and, above all, purposeful, as opposed to being change for the sake of change. This is why leaders who are effective in casting vision will also be conservationists. That is, they will not only paint pictures of a more enticing future, but they will also learn to affirm and celebrate what is good in the past and present of a church, being clear about what needs to change but being equally clear about what is not, at the moment at least, on the agenda for change.

Clarity of purpose is vital, of course, not simply as we embark upon the change process, but also as we continue on as a church. I know of no church, and of no leader, which is not bombarded with far more mission and ministry opportunities than it has the resources for, and a bewildering array of competing demands for time, people, and energy. Being fuelled and shaped by a clear vision means that a church is able to discern more easily what are the appropriate demands on resources to which it should respond and what demands are inappropriate or not essential. Vision clarifies who we are, helps us answer the question of why we are here and what would be lost if we were not here, and keeps us from being distracted.[14]

## Fostering unity

One thing that has the greatest potential to rein in the entrepreneurial spirit of any leader is the fear of provoking disharmony or disunity. It is also a common fear of many church members who see even the slightest hint of unhappiness on the part of any other member as an indication that the changes which have provoked that unhappiness must automatically be flawed or wrong. This is probably why many churches end up as functional democracies in which majority opinion holds sway and in which any change is resisted until we can guarantee that everyone will agree to it.

Research suggests that, although people embrace change at different speeds, and most people might eventually adopt new initiatives, a proportion of people (perhaps as many as 5–10 per cent) will *never* embrace any change. It is not difficult, therefore, to see why many churches end up stuck in inertia and decline. Given that people tend to be complex and to differ from one another in various ways, even in a church where change is resisted out of fear of provoking conflict there is no guarantee that discord and disunity will not be a familiar experience. The history of ecumenical movements is that where unity is pursued as a goal in itself it is very rarely achieved other than on a very superficial basis. However, where churches and groups gather around a common task or goal, there is a high probability that trivial differences can be set aside and a high level of unity and harmony can be accomplished. In a local church setting, new vision may well be disturbing initially and may provoke a wide variety of responses, from instant acceptance to downright rejection. There is, however, good evidence to suggest that a shared vision may well be the one thing that ultimately works to unite an otherwise disparate and diverse congregation around a common mission.

It's hard to imagine a more diverse group of people than that which Jesus gathered around Himself as His first apostles. It was a remarkable achievement, and a risky one at that, to draw together strongly minded liberationists such as Simon the Zealot and Judas Iscariot – who must, at least, have flirted with the fringes of radical terrorist groups – alongside those such as Matthew who, as a tax collector, must have been seen by them as collaborators with the Roman army of occupation. That they functioned so well together both alongside Jesus during His earthly ministry and also in leading His church after His ascension is profound witness to the potency of the kingdom vision which Jesus cast and which drew them together in common cause. If we want to see our churches hold together and share a common mind, then we need to cast clear vision; it is the only thing with the capacity to facilitate true unity.

## Stimulating action

When I came to my current church I took over leadership of a congregation of people who were weary and somewhat dispirited and who had seen their numbers decline significantly in recent times. Although I fairly quickly began to discern what I felt to be an appropriate way forward for the church, for all kinds of reasons it would have been quite inappropriate and totally counterproductive simply to impose a new vision upon them. I chose, very early on, to take a group of twelve key leaders away for the day and to help them explore with me the vision I felt God was giving us in terms of our future. I was especially concerned about the response of one or two, whom I suspected might be the most resistant but whom I judged to be critical in terms of getting others on board. At the end of a fairly lengthy day of inputting and processing together, I finally asked people for any personal response to what had been shared. There was silence until one of the two spoke up: "When do we start?" he asked. He became one of the key champions of the vision and one of my most energetic practitioners in terms of seeing that vision come to fruition. As George Verwer puts it: "Vision is a powerful sense of what needs to be done and the initiative to take hold of it and work towards its completion."[15]

## DISCERNING VISION

Leaders have a key role to play in the vision process. However, this is neither to suggest that leaders have a monopoly when it comes to discerning vision for a church, nor is it to imply that a visionary leader is necessarily an especially original thinker who regularly has seventeen new ideas before breakfast. Bennis and Nanus helpfully point out that:

> *Historians tend to write about great leaders as if they possessed transcendent genius... but upon closer examination it usually turns out that the vision did not originate with the leader personally but rather from others...*
>
> *... the leader may have been the one who chose the image from those available at the moment, articulated it, gave it form and legitimacy, and focused attention on it, but the leader only rarely was the one who conceived of the vision in the first place. Therefore the leader must be a superb listener... Successful leaders are great askers, and they do pay attention.[16]*

## Listening to God

In the first place, the visionary leader listens to God and to His story. Shawchuck and Heuser suggest that:

> *Vision is a mystical happening dreamed in the hearts of God's servants by the Spirit. Vision cannot be planned, only received from God. As such, vision always comes from beyond us and outside of our context, and it is always larger than life.*[17]

A vision for the local church will be informed by and will arise from the kind of understanding of God's design for His people which we explored in an earlier chapter. It will be a more specific and contextual outworking of such a purpose and serves to animate and transform purpose into action. To arrive at this in the first place, the visionary leader needs to ensure that they are so immersed in the biblical narrative of God's dealings with His people that their imagination is stirred in terms of what God might wish to do now and in the future with this specific congregation of His people entrusted to them.

Richard Niebuhr observes, "The great Christian revolutions came not by the discovery of something that was not known before. They happen when someone takes radically something that was always there."[18] Nehemiah was so taken with the purposes God still had for His people and with the terms of the covenant by which He had committed himself to those people that he did not find it difficult to envision what the future might look like for that people. Secular studies suggest that the most effective leaders when it comes to imagining what the future might look like are those who are able to reflect on the past and to attend to the present. Reflection on the past enlarges our understanding of future possibilities. Noticing what is going on right now in other places highlights patterns of activity which might be replicated in our own context.

So, in addition to reflecting on God's great works in history, secondly we take note of His current activities. Experience of, or at least familiarity with, contemporary stories of God's working in the world fuel our imagination as to what He might do here and serve to stimulate vision. One of the great weaknesses of much contemporary denominational positional leadership is the proportion of people occupying those positions who have never had significant first-hand experience of seeing churches grow and the kingdom advance. Little wonder that their approach has been, at best, to maintain what they are stewarding and, at worst, to manage decline. By contrast, one of the most helpful things we can do in order to commend ownership of vision is to tell stories of God's activity.[19]

## Listening to my context

Visionary leaders listen to God and also pay attention to the realities of the situation that they face; they listen to their context. Vision is never abstract or disembodied, nor is it an "off the peg" replication of what someone else is doing to good effect in another place. It is always specific to the context out of which it arises, and it emerges out of an imagining of that context in the light of the missional narrative of God. The first thing that Nehemiah does on reaching Jerusalem is – under the cover of darkness to maintain some secrecy – to inspect the city walls in order to gain an accurate assessment of the reality of the situation that faces him. When he then begins to cast vision, he is able to refer directly to this reality and thus his vision has real cogency as opposed to being merely wishful thinking.

When we moved to Saltburn, I did something I have never done before or since in church leadership: I spent several weeks visiting, in their homes, as many as possible of the people who identified themselves as church members. I asked each of them two questions. First I asked how long they had been part of Emmanuel Church, giving them opportunity to open up about their feelings about the church. Then I asked how they had come to faith and how their faith had grown, giving me some idea as to the level of spiritual vitality among church members. This also helped to show who might be the most spiritually open and hungry and thus most favourably disposed to whatever new thing God might want to do among us. It was this "fact-finding" mission which informed my subsequent vision-casting and which gave me some indication as to the nature and size of the task ahead. It was invaluable. We can save ourselves a good deal of time and spare ourselves the frustration of false starts in a new place if we give a few weeks over simply to getting the true feel of a place.

## Listening to others

The other benefit of taking time to engage especially with those whom it will be most important to get on board with new vision is that it communicates that you take their perspectives seriously and builds a level of trust capital with them, which will serve you well going forward. So, thirdly, effective leaders listen to other people within the church. Kouzes and Posner observe that:

> The best leaders... listen carefully to what other people have to say and how they feel. They have to ask good questions, be open to ideas other than their own, and even lose arguments in favour of the common good. Through intense listening, leaders get a sense of what people want, what they value, and what they dream about.[20]

This is not for one moment to suggest that vision is simply a collage of the various aspirations of different church members. Rather, it is a recognition that others may actually have something to contribute to the vision process. Others also have an ability to hear from God and to be led by Him, and they understand the specific community and context in which the vision is to be worked out. It also takes seriously the fact that for some, at least, it is very important that they feel part of the vision-forming process, rather than having it imposed on them. This gives people the opportunity to feel more of a shared ownership of the vision for the future, from a shared starting point, and so enables them to buy into it fully.

One exercise I have found useful, especially with leadership teams who have some level of formation through engagement with God's missional story (and thus whose contributions can be relied upon to be not simply expressions of personal preference), is to get them to describe their own preferred future for the mission and ministry of our church. One of the very early exercises I engaged in with the then leadership team in my current church was to get them all to write a letter to our former associate vicar who had just left to take up another appointment. I wrote the first two lines, which read simply:

*Dear John,*

*Can it really be five years since you moved on from Marple? You wouldn't believe what has happened over those five years here. Let me tell you about a few of the things we have seen take place...*

Each staff member had to complete their own letter to John, and then read it aloud to the rest of the team at a staff awayday. We then compiled a long list of the various dreams that had been expressed, agreed together which ones were either inappropriate or unrealistic, and then spent the rest of the day working out which were legitimate aspirations. At the end of the day we had a number of different general and specific things we agreed we longed to see come about. Although some were very ambitious, within three years virtually all of them had been achieved.

It goes without saying that the higher people's level of commitment to the life of the church and their engagement with its governance, the greater their expectation of being involved in the discerning of vision for its future. This has profound implications for the way in which we cast and commend such vision to the church and to its different constituent groups.

## CASTING VISION

It is one thing to have been captivated oneself by a vision for God's work, but until such vision becomes embedded widely in the life and consciousness of a church it remains just a dream in the mind of the leader. The experience of Nehemiah reminds us that the more compelling such a vision is to us and the more we allow ourselves to be consumed by it, the more determined and effective we are likely to be in communicating and commending it.[21]

Not only did I spend a good deal of time, in my early weeks in Saltburn, surveying the lie of the land, but I also gave time to fasting and prayer, and spent hours prayer-walking the community. I tried to allow God to impress more deeply upon me His heart and mind for our church and community, and to grow in me a passion for seeing this come about. Now came the time to begin to seek to get others on board.

## Co-discerning with positional leaders

Those with positional leadership in a traditional church will not necessarily be those who will ultimately be the greatest champions of a fresh vision or those who will be most skilled at commending it to others (as we have previously noted, position does not imply influence). However, it is difficult, in the early stages at least, to make any progress in the vision-casting process, without beginning with such people. Given that I was leading an Anglican church, this meant, for me, working with the PCC.

The first step I took was to take the PCC away for a day to take a good look at where we were as a church. I entitled the day "Is my church worth joining?", tapping into a fairly uncontroversial aspiration that most people had of seeing our church grow numerically and its decline halted. I began by leading the PCC in an exploration of the key features of the early church as presented in the opening chapters of the Acts of the Apostles. I did some broad-based Bible teaching, to give a lead for the subsequent discussion. Then I got them, in groups, to engage with some biblical texts and to come up with a list of key qualities and features which we saw as integral to the church as God intends it. The whole purpose of this exercise was to try to cultivate our missional imagination as we reconnected with the story of God, and to steer things away from any notion of "the new vicar's ideas about how our church should change" and onto what it really means for us to be the church of Jesus Christ. Stephen Cottrell points out that:

> *It is highly desirable that the leader should have the odd dazzlingly brilliant insight, but the more important quality is the willingness to recall the organisation to its primary vocation... It is the task*

*of leadership to articulate vision and endlessly recall the community or organisation to its fundamental purpose and values.*[22]

Tapping into the core DNA of the kingdom began to bring to the surface a buried and perhaps forgotten memory of what the church was truly about. We went on to analyse which of these essential qualities were authentically expressed in the life of our church, which were missing, and what we might do in order to come more into line with God's will for us. The exercise had potency because it consisted in all of us submitting ourselves to the narrative of Scripture, co-discerning the mind of Christ, as opposed to one person seeking to impose vision on the others. Not everyone was completely happy with the outcome of the day, and many felt more than a little uncomfortable, but most were persuaded of the validity of our conclusions. This provided a foundation for forward movement.

## Identifying the engine drivers

James Lawrence presents a model[23] which I have found immensely helpful over the years in understanding the dynamics of the vision communication process. Using an image from the world of transport, he likens four distinct constituencies within the church to four different groups of people on the railways.

- Radicals (tracklayers) are those who have high aspirations for change, and who are often visionary and innovative thinkers. They lay the track without which a train cannot move, but by the time we catch up with them, they are usually around the next corner!

- Progressives (engine drivers) are the early adopters who are enthusiastic about change, are aware that it needs wisdom to see it through, usually get their ideas from the Radicals (they run on the track laid by the tracklayers), but also are sensitive to how Conservatives will respond.

- Conservatives (fare-paying passengers) are the late adopters who are innately conservative and suspicious of change but who can be persuaded to get on board if they feel that their concerns and feelings are taken seriously.

- Traditionalists (brake van) may well be the never adopters who fear that all change is for the worse and undermines the past. They may have a positive role to play in bringing a check and balance to the unrestrained enthusiasm of the tracklayers, but most of us would like to cast the brake van adrift most of the time!

The most helpful insight for me from this model is that the ones who provide the motive power for getting vision embedded and seeing change come about are not the tracklayers but the engine drivers. They are the key influencers of the vast majority. These are the people who quickly own the vision and commend and explain it to others such that others begin to embrace it. So, one of the key tasks for a leader of change, especially one who is primarily a tracklayer, is to identify the engine drivers. In a more mature church these might be the small group leaders and heads of ministry areas among others. Part of my aim in visiting the church membership extensively in my early weeks in Saltburn was to identify the spiritually open and hungry whom, I guessed, might prove to be potential engine drivers.

Having identified them, I then began to gather them in an arena in which they might be shaped and equipped to inhabit the vision. This was probably not going to happen principally within the context of Sunday worship or other existing activities. After two months in post we launched a midweek gathering in our home, simply entitled "Open to God", to which anyone was welcome but to which I made a point of specifically inviting those who were potential "engine drivers". These meetings consisted of simple sung worship, reflection around Scripture, and informal prayer, all of which were something of a novelty to those attending!

The first meeting drew around fifteen people, but eventually it began to grow. Within three years it had not only tripled in size but had become the spiritual heart of the church, and a place where people grew in their understanding of God, in their encounter with Him, and in being equipped to exercise influence for Him. For those who are serious about seeing the culture of a church changed, the establishing of such a group in which people can be effectively formed should be a top priority, and we will look more at this in Chapter 7. For us, it felt a little like planting a culture within a church which would ultimately permeate the whole church and shape and redefine the whole.

## Communicating it widely

If the engine drivers are to be able to commend the vision, then the wider church community need to have a clear understanding of what is being commended and reinforced. Much of my preaching and teaching in my first year was around an understanding of the Christian good news, of the calling and identity of the church, and the meaning of discipleship. It sought to answer questions to do with who we are and what we are called to do as a local church.

It's a good idea to take every opportunity to reinforce and underline these broad ideas through, for instance, monthly bulletins, reports to PCC, and in personal conversation with others. In our current church, we have three regular, annual occasions[24] when we reiterate core vision and celebrate things that have happened that serve to further such vision. All of us have short memories and require frequent reminders around core vision!

The communication of vision needs to be clear, which is why often a pithy vision statement or set of simple and memorable core values are really important for a church to adopt. But it also needs to be compelling, and for this two particular qualities are essential.

Vision needs to connect with the aspirations and longings of those to whom we are seeking to communicate it. Donna Ladkin[25] suggests that a crucial aspect of a successful leadership vision is the extent to which it aligns meaning for those involved in a common activity. People commit to a vision when they begin to see how it enables the accomplishment of the things that ultimately matter to them.

A friend of mine demonstrated this skill brilliantly when he was raising money for a church refurbishment scheme which involved, among other things, replacing pews with chairs and creating a more flexible space in his church building. Although this was a popular move in many quarters in the church, he knew that he would face resistance from one particular, traditional group of, mainly elderly, worshippers. Many had grown up in this same church and had raised families in the community. He asked how many had children or grandchildren who were still actively involved in local churches. Few had. When asked why that was, several explained that those children did not have family-orientated churches in the areas in which they now lived. If only there was a church near them, like this church, with lots of activities for children and families, then perhaps they might still attend.

My friend sympathized that these worshippers could no longer do anything to help their own children in this way, but what about the other parents and grandparents around the country who had children and grandchildren living in our community? Wouldn't it be great to be able to do something to help them? He then explained how the refurbishment programme was, in part, to facilitate wider ministry to children and young people. Within twenty minutes one of the congregation was on his doorstep, instinctively opposed to the reordering of a beloved building, but with a substantial cheque towards the costs of buying chairs! When we cast vision we need to make sure that we tap into people's emotions and feelings and not simply their minds, and help people see how it affects what is of ultimate importance to them.

Finally, people are far more likely to commit to a vision when they see the passion it arouses in the person commending it. When we ourselves demonstrate that we are sold out for something, others are far more likely to join us in it. We cannot take others further than we have journeyed ourselves, and we cannot expect higher levels of commitment from others than we are prepared to invest ourselves. Trust is a vital component in visionary leadership, and that trust is in part generated by a recognition of passion and investment on the part of the leader. Other people will be more able to invest in the vision when they are able to catch our passionate enthusiasm and draw energy from that.

People want leaders who are realistic about the situation in which we find ourselves but equally who are able to communicate hope by being upbeat, optimistic, and positive about the future. Only then can we expect them to follow us willingly to a place they have not yet visited.

## FURTHER READING

Warren Bennis and Burt Nanus, *Leaders*, New York: Harper Collins, 2007

James Kouzes and Barry Posner, *The Leadership Challenge*, San Francisco, CA: Jossey-Bass, 2012

Peter M. Senge, *The Fifth Discipline*, London: Random House, 2006

# Useful Vision-Casting Exercises

1. Ask each member of your team to write a letter (possibly to a former colleague who has recently moved on) dated five years in the future, in which they describe some of the things which have taken place since the departure of that colleague.

Dear John,

Can it really be five years since you moved on from us? You wouldn't believe what has happened over the course of the last five years! Let me describe a few of the new initiatives we have taken...

2. Ask each team member to answer the following question:

"If you could start anything you wanted to, with all the resources you might need, and with success guaranteed, what three things might you do?"

3. Imagine that Jesus joined your church six months ago. Describe some of the things He has been doing and getting you to do with Him over the course of the last six months.

or

If Jesus came to your community today, where might you find Him, who would He be with, and how would He spend His time?

## Values Brainstorm

Sometimes the key thing for a church is to agree upon a set of shared values which will determine the way in which it conducts its life and ministry. A useful exercise to help people form a clear value statement is as follows:

- *Give each person a list of around fifty values. Ask each person to highlight the top eight which she feels are most important for the church and to which she is most willing to commit. People may add other values to the list if they feel that an essential value has been omitted.*

- *In groups of four, each person shares their own list and the group agrees on five core values and upon a definition of each one.*

- *Each group shares its findings with the wider team and particular trends are noted.*

- *The whole team agrees on four or five core values for the church, and the congregation can then be given an opportunity to reflect in small groups or in other ways on both the agreed values, and on what it might mean to live out these values in every aspect of the church's life.*

# 4

## Holding On Tight:
## Leading Through Transitions

We know that managing people and organisations
through times of tumultuous change is one of the
most difficult tasks a leader faces. We are beginning
to get glimmers of the future, but there are still many
unknowns and much uncertainty. During such times a
leader might be tempted to take short cuts, to focus on
new vehicles for accomplishing quick results. We caution
against such tactics.[1]

When I set out for the first time on the journey
of leading a church through significant change
I supposed that, having seen the church
launched reasonably painlessly on that journey, the course
it would follow would be a fairly consistent one. If I had
plotted it in advance on a graph, I would very likely have
drawn it as a straight line, or at least as a smooth, ascending
curve. Four years on, I was about to experience something
of a reality check!

Having witnessed significant changes to the culture of the
church over four years, and having seen lots of positive things
come about — including numbers of people coming to faith,
direct giving more than doubling, some freeing up of Sunday
worship — it seemed to me that we had weathered the initial
storms of change and were now positioned to be able to

really move forward with the church, and its leadership, on board with the new vision.

I had planned a PCC awayday with the purpose of beginning to discern together and then formulate a mission strategy for the next period in the church's life. It ended up being just about the most difficult day I experienced in the whole of my nine years in Saltburn! There were a good number of people who were wholly behind the new things that had taken place. However, I hadn't quite realized how many were feeling more than a little nervous at the pace of change, and who were also probably aware of friends (especially those in the "brake van"[2]) who were very unhappy at what was happening to "their" church. All these fears and anxieties began to surface on the awayday. People talked about experiencing a "divided" church; some wanted to return, at least in part, to former ways of doing things; and whatever joy there might have been over the positive gains we had seen over the last years was eclipsed by apprehension over a still uncertain future.

In retrospect, a number of factors were probably coming into play. Initial enthusiasm for a new way, which held out the promise of hope and vitality for the church, was now being tempered by an understanding of the actual costs involved. People were beginning to grieve over the loss of some things which had been more precious than they had realized. Leaving behind an existence which was predictable, and in which people felt in control of things, for the sake of a far more uncertain future in which we were consciously seeking to give control over to God, suddenly felt very scary. Most significantly, there was probably a realization that the changes in form and culture which had come about over the last few years were actually here to stay. This was not some temporary adventure, after the end of which things would return to normal, but rather the new reality which was here to stay.

This insight has led me to conclude that the most challenging time for those involved in leading churches through changes may well not be the initial stages of the process, but rather the intermediate stages. Our rockiest ride may well come in years three to five. You have been warned! Whatever the reasons, the Saltburn PCC awayday seemed to be overtaken by an outpouring of reservations, anxieties, and expressions of other unhappiness.

It would have been very easy simply to take this merely as a personal attack on my leadership (it was, at least, in part) and to respond by justifying myself and the way I had led over the previous four years. In the fortnight that followed I was certainly tempted to do this (and probably lay awake a few nights mentally composing letters and other position papers!). It was the only occasion in the whole of my time in Saltburn when I ever considered the possibility of leaving to take on something less disheartening (the overwhelming sense of being called by God to Emmanuel Church prevented me from doing anything about it!).

It was the time when I learned, however, some key lessons concerning effective leadership through times of transitions. It became obvious to me that the progress of change is rarely consistent; it might more accurately be drawn as a kind of saw-tooth line on a graph. I also discovered that initiating change is probably a whole lot easier than leading through times of transition, and that the key to seeing lasting change accomplished actually lies in the way we help people navigate their way through the rather choppier waters in the middle of transitions.

Once again, Nehemiah was a good friend and a wise counsellor. After the initial enthusiasm of the people to rebuild the walls of Jerusalem, and after they had launched themselves into the enterprise, Nehemiah faced, in many ways, his most significant challenges. As the rebuilding starts to take shape, Nehemiah's enemies begin to make threats in such a way that both those involved in the building work, but especially other Jews living in the vicinity,[3] begin to lose heart and are consumed with fear. The cost involved in the work doesn't seem worth a benefit which is, as yet, still over the horizon. Not only do these opponents seek to disturb the rank and file inhabitants of the city, but they also do their best to distract Nehemiah and to besmirch his character, reputation, and motives. This is, in many ways, the most critical phase of the rebuilding in terms of its future success. It is vital that Nehemiah not only conducts himself well but also leads his people effectively through this tricky period. The key to this, I discovered during my own tricky time in Saltburn, is holding your nerve, and coaching others to do the same.

In his wonderfully helpful book on change management, *Managing Transitions*, William Bridges highlights the difference between *change* and *transition*. The former, he suggests, is situational. It may, in a church context, consist in a change in worship pattern, in leadership structure, in the adoption of a new mission statement or set of core values. It can be described in terms of a clear before and after. Transition is a far more complex phenomenon and is more to do with people's ownership of and internalization of the change process and of the new reality that it introduces.

It was the complexities of this process which were the cause of the difficulties which surfaced on our awayday. Bridges suggests that transition is, in fact, a three-phase process which is essential to the eventual success of the change becoming established. Each phase comes with its own unique challenges and difficulties. The secret to moving any organization forward into a new reality is to lead transition well. This, he suggests, involves helping people through three phases.[4]

## 1. THE ENDING

This phase is all about letting go of old ways and the old identity people had. Although people might agree intellectually or rationally to the need for something to end in order for something new to begin, it often takes quite a while for people's hearts to catch up with their heads. And often it is not until we have embarked upon an agreed process of change that we fully realize the emotional and personal implications of that change. We may agree in principle that public worship ought to be designed in such a way that unchurched people might find it accessible. But after a few months of inhabiting a new worship regime, we may begin to long for the reassuring familiarity of what we once had, and even resent the new people who have been enabled to find a home in our church because of the new approach. It takes a while for people to come to terms with endings, and this phase may well be characterized by feelings of loss and all the emotions which traditionally accompany bereavement.

During this phase, the wise leader will empathize with people in their loss. One good strategy is to try to understand exactly who has lost what and to demonstrate your understanding of some of the emotions they are now experiencing. Trying to minimize the loss which others are suffering, or encouraging people to be upbeat, or trying to emphasize the positive gains which have resulted from the new reality, are all strategies which may well compound the sense of loss and which may lead people to distance themselves from you and your leadership. What people need most is understanding, even if that understanding is accompanied by a steadfast refusal to compromise in terms of the future direction of the church.

In this phase, when increasingly your leadership is being

characterized by what you are changing, it is probably also important to draw attention to what you are *not* changing and why. As Peter Senge puts it:

> *Change naturally induces fear in us all: fear of the unknown, of failure, of not being needed in a new order of things. When we obsessively focus on what needs to be changed, and not on what we intend to conserve, we reinforce those fears. But when we can clarify what we intend to conserve, some of this fear can be released.*[5]

Celebrating and affirming that which has been fruitful and valued in the recent life of a local church, and committing your support for its future, brings reassurance. Innovations can then be presented as developments that build on the past and help to realize its potential.[6]

> *The single biggest reason organisational changes fail is that... planners and implementers all too often forget that people have to let go of the present first. They forget that while the first task of change management is to understand the desired outcome and how to get there, the first task of transition management is to convince people to leave home. You'll save yourself a lot of grief if you remember that.*[7]

## 2. THE NEUTRAL ZONE

Bridges suggests that this phase is a time when all the old clarities break down and everything is in flux. It is a profoundly ambiguous time when people are aware of having left something familiar behind in search of something attractive but as yet unknown, but are equally aware that the new reality has not yet come into being. The growing sense of loss has little to compensate for it. Moreover, the difficulty of this phase is compounded by the fact that many people do not realize that this phase actually exists, assuming that it is possible to move swiftly from the death of one thing to the birth of another.

This is, of course, the critical phase in which new identity, practice, and strategy is being formed and internalized by people. It is vital that people be nurtured and coached well through it and helped to form such new identity. This is a time to put a hold on any additional change initiatives. Yet more uncertainty will merely unsettle those who are on the journey and will prejudice the success of the major changes whose transition you are currently managing. The years ahead in Saltburn were years in which some of the most significant structural and strategic changes took place. What became clear at the PCC awayday, however, was that the introduction of fresh initiatives at this stage – that is, before the previous changes became thoroughly internalized – would prejudice the completion of what was, in effect, an unfinished journey.

This is the time when people will need the reassurance of a leader who has a clearer grasp than they on the future towards which we are heading. When the people of Jerusalem find themselves in their own "neutral zone", Nehemiah reminds them of the sure hope which they have in the Lord and reassures them of God's good purposes for them.[8] In this season, we need to be dealers in hope, and we need to continually articulate the vision which has drawn us forward to this place. This is a time to tell stories of hope and to celebrate the things which we are seeing God do among us.

This is an uncomfortable time for the leader as well as for those whom he or she is seeking to lead. Leaders are anxious to see things progress and people move forward as rapidly as possible. Time spent explaining (again!) the reasons for change and offering reassurance can seem to be time wasted. The temptation is always to turn a blind eye to the uncertainty that people are experiencing, or to pretend that people are further on than they really are in terms of the journey. That may well have been my mistake during this difficult phase of our ministry in Saltburn.

Patrick Lencioni, in his classic leadership fable *The Five Dysfunctions of a Team*,[9] highlights fear of conflict as one of the greatest threats to the health of a team or, for that matter, any other organization. Conflict is, essentially, the articulation of difference or of disagreement. If it is not articulated, then disagreement is suppressed but does not actually disappear. Rather, it tends to surface in more destructive forms and leads to unhelpful tension. Lencioni suggests that the wise leader will "mine" for conflict – that is, provide safe opportunities for people to express reservations or disagreements, and for these to be processed constructively. Often people's unhappiness arises not primarily from a specific issue in and of itself but from the fact that they fear that their opinion on this issue is not being heard.

## 3. THE NEW BEGINNING

It is not straightforward to determine when this phase actually arrives, mainly because different people will enter it at different times. Figure 1 may well be familiar to some already and is a helpful illustration of this phenomenon.

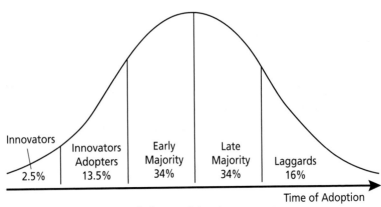

Figure 1 The Bell Curve of Change Adoption

Some will have jumped into it almost immediately after the initial vision was sown (these people are sometimes referred to as "innovators" or "radicals"); others will have got on board quickly (early adopters). Many will have done so gradually (early majority); some will get there eventually (late majority), while others will never embrace change at all (laggards/resisters). It is probably fair to say that the new beginning has properly arrived when a good number of the late majority are on board. Some people assume that the process is complete when the "early majority" have bought in (this was probably my mistake). The most critical period may well be the final stages of helping those who are moving more slowly to embrace the changes. This is not to say, by the way, that you should waste too much time and effort in trying to get "laggards" on board. They might never be persuaded, or even helped, to embrace change. They need to be loved, and politely worked around!

Measuring the right time to initiate specific changes is an important discipline. Mastering it will save time and emotional energy. It is a reasonable assumption that a new minister will have a certain amount of capital in his or her account with the church and will be able to effect some minor changes almost straightaway. An older and wiser friend suggested to me as I was about to move to our new church that I make at least one very visible but fairly inconsequential change immediately, in order to indicate that there was a new regime in place (to that very end, he had painted the doors of his church building a completely different colour upon arriving there!). I decided to get rid of the elaborate robes which had traditionally been worn by ministers at Emmanuel Church, and negotiated that privilege from the churchwardens as a condition of my accepting the job. I actually didn't have any complaints about it beyond my very first service there, but it did serve to alert people to the fact that it was not simply "business as usual". That said, when it comes to effecting more significant and meaningful change, it is vital to wait until you can be sure of a reasonable consensus among those who have responsibility for decision-making.

When I arrived in Saltburn there were all manner of things that I recognized as needing to change if the long-term spiritual health of the church was to be guaranteed. However, I also recognized that it would be futile to strike too soon if I wanted a reasonable chance of success in terms of managing change. One of my principal concerns which I identified almost immediately was the church's approach to raising money and an over-reliance on fundraising in order to pay the bills. One of my biggest bugbears was the prize draw which was made every month over coffee after Sunday worship. I have a strong aversion to anything which bears any resemblance to gambling, and, more importantly, well understood that the idea of *raising* money was inimical to the development of a culture of generosity and giving.

However, it would have been entirely counterproductive to tackle this head-on straight away, and, although people were well aware that this was something about which I was uncomfortable, I actually did nothing about it for three years. After three years, during which time I had preached regularly on the subject of money, giving, and generosity, and during which time regular financial giving to the church had doubled, I simply proposed to the PCC that we put an end to the prize draw. There wasn't even a murmur of opposition.

## FIVE DO'S AND DON'TS FOR LEADING THROUGH TRANSITIONS

### 1. Don't assume followers are travelling at the same pace as you

All of us have probably experienced that sense of shock when the train on which we are travelling goes into a tunnel, often accompanied, in my experience, with the huge frustration of suddenly finding that the phone call we were making has been cut off because we have lost connection with any mobile phone signal! What has been shocking and disorientating for us has been an entirely different experience for the train driver. The driver knew exactly what was coming, experienced the tunnel a little ahead of us, and could see the circle of light steadily growing larger, which indicates that the tunnel would shortly come to an end.

In the same way, different people will not only embrace change at different paces to one another, but will be at different stages in terms of understanding what the change journey feels like. Too many leaders — and I have certainly been guilty of this — assume that just because we have a clear overview of the journey and understand where we are at the present time, and just because we have communicated such an overview once or twice to the wider congregation, then everyone will automatically be at the same place as we are ourselves. This is reinforced by the fact that some people actually are alongside us on the journey and may even be straining to press ahead of us. We can never over-communicate when it comes to articulating vision and describing the way forward.

More importantly, even those who might have a reasonable understanding of the trajectory the church is following may well be lagging behind the leader in terms of emotions and feelings. The leader has probably come to terms with the emotional cost of change. They have passed through the dark and cold tunnel of loss and have now surged forward into the warmth of daylight. Others may still be passing through the tunnel, living with the reality of feeling the pain of loss, experiencing a measure of confusion and frustration, and with little sight, as yet, of the sure hope which the future promises. We need to help people pass through these times and not appear impatient with or critical of those who have not yet travelled as far as we have.

The journey of the Israelites through the wilderness following their dramatic escape from Egypt is a helpful metaphor for understanding this process. They had experienced God's remarkable deliverance in the exodus. However, in the weeks that followed – especially when the desert place in which they found themselves seemed so inhospitable – we find them grumbling about their situation, about their leadership, and even reminiscing with nostalgic affection for what they had left behind in Egypt. The familiar, even if harsh, can appear more attractive than the unknown. Moses has a clear picture of the land which God has promised and to which he is seeking to lead the people. He has to keep on painting compelling pictures of this land in order to move the people forward. In these times we will do well to try to sit where our people are sitting, to understand the experiences they are undergoing, and to help them continue to move forward.

## 2. Do be prepared to live with mess

The transition period is usually one which is hallmarked by uncertainty and mess. Solid gains live cheek by jowl with frustrations and disappointments. Clarity in terms of vision and values may well be accompanied by lack of certainty in terms of strategies and plans for seeing such vision come to fruition.

Mike Bonem helpfully, if rather uncomfortably, points out:

> It is a mistake to think that God will unveil a complete plan before starting a process of transformation. Throughout the book of Acts, Paul and other leaders stepped out in faith without knowing where the journey would lead. Joshua is a vivid example of another change agent who led with an incomplete road map... I believe that Christian leadership may be filled with even more short-term uncertainty than secular leadership because God wants us to learn to be dependent upon Him, not on our own plans, and to demonstrate this dependence to others.[10]

People find mess uncomfortable. You will probably have more than a few people in your church who will want to point out their opinion that mess and uncertainty is a sign that things are not right and that the sooner you sort things out and restore some form of predictable order the better. There is an emotional cost to uncertainty. However, any change process will always include significant periods of uncertainty, and such times should not be short-circuited, for two very good reasons. Firstly, the only sure way to avoid such uncertainty is to retreat, which is counterproductive.

But secondly, it is actually such uncertainty which ultimately generates the motivation and the energy to move forward.

In his helpful exploration of this phenomenon, Peter Senge[11] suggests that moments in which we experience a gap between vision and reality are moments in which we experience two conflicting sources of tension. Emotional tension, which arises out of a sense of discouragement over our current state, leads to the temptation to lighten the load by redefining or reducing the scope of the vision. In organizations, he suggests, goals erode because of low tolerance for emotional tension:

> The easiest path is to pretend that there is no bad news or, easier still, just declare victory – to redefine the bad news as not so bad by lowering the standard against which it is judged. Escaping emotional tension is easy – the only price we pay is abandoning what we truly want, our vision.[12]

For many people in contexts of uncertainty, the cost of pressing on towards seeing the vision fulfilled is seen as less worthwhile than a return to a sense of peace and harmony and a consequent abandonment of at least some aspects of the desired future.

However, Senge points out that there is another form of tension which can be harnessed for the purpose of seeing the vision accomplished:

> Imagine a rubber band stretched between your vision and current reality. When stretched, the rubber band creates tension, representing the tension between vision and current reality. What does tension seek? resolution or release. There are only two possible ways for tension to resolve itself: pull reality towards the vision or pull the vision towards reality. Which occurs will depend on whether we hold steady to the vision.

*Truly creative people use the gap between vision and current reality to generate energy for change.*[13]

One way of seeing such energy generated is to remind people of the "problems" we are facing (for example, difficulty in reaching unchurched people, young families, lack of connectedness with our community), which have themselves occasioned our search for fresh vision. When we reiterate the reasons for our fresh vision, then we stimulate in people a longing for change and allow the tension they experience in the present to be the energy which drives forward momentum towards such change coming about.

## 3. Don't personalize

People need to vent their unhappiness and, given that you have been at the epicentre of the process that has caused them grief, you may well find yourself in the line of fire. Things may be said subtly and indirectly, but you'll be left in little doubt that you are being held responsible for what is causing pain.

We have choices in terms of how we deal with people's outpourings. Our instinct is often to try to justify ourselves or to defend ourselves, which often leads us into engaging with people on the same kind of emotional level with which they have addressed us. This is rarely, if ever, productive. It may leave us feeling justified and we may feel that we have had the better of an argument. But not only does it tend to make others feel put down and even more bruised, it may well result in people becoming more entrenched in their own hurt and damaged feelings, and also inhibit them from expressing their feelings openly in the future. This only pushes dissent underground and means that it will issue forth in more covert and potentially destructive ways in the future.

I am by no means advocating turning a blind eye to expressions of unhappiness. It is usually important to acknowledge how people are feeling. However, it is very important to avoid personalizing such feelings. The only way we can effectively do this is to keep our own eyes fixed on the road ahead. This is exactly what Nehemiah does. When faced with attacks on his reputation, threats to his safety and that of those working with him, rumours, questioning, the fears of those who have signed up to work alongside him and who are now wavering in confidence, his refrain is always simply that he is engaged in a great work and cannot be distracted from it. He processes all of this with God, and reflects before God on the actions and intentions of those who wish to do him harm. God is a safe person with whom to do such reflecting. It helps, too, to have someone closer at hand – but out of the immediate context in which we are working – to whom we can unburden ourselves, express our own feelings, and do some processing of our experiences and their impact upon us. It helps us to maintain a balanced perspective.

## 4. Don't look down

One of the things I admire most as I look at Nehemiah's career is his refusal to compromise his convictions and his determination to bring his plans to a conclusion, even in the face of significant opposition. Even the most resilient leader faces the spectres of self-doubt and something of a crisis in self-confidence when having to deal with repeated challenges. The temptation to reduce the scope of the original vision in order to placate your most resolute opponents is seductive and very real. The energy required to persevere with the plans that you have dreamed with God, and yet which some others find so difficult, is significant, and the prospect of toning things down just for the sake of an easier life often seems attractive. There will be plenty of voices suggesting that your plans might be too ambitious, certainly for this church at this time. How about scaling things back? There will be people who will want to bargain with you for a restoration of cherished ways of doing things. Others will want to tell you about the risks you are running in terms of alienating people if you carry on as you have been doing.

One of the qualities which the New Testament seems to value especially highly is that of endurance or perseverance. Put simply, it is the determination to press on and to see through that which God has entrusted to us no matter what threats and challenges come our way. One of the leadership axioms that we seem to have developed in my current church is a phrase we use to spur one another on especially while in the middle of transitions and when faced with pressure to compromise: *Don't look down*. It's a reminder to keep looking ahead, knowing that as we do so, and as we continue to move forward step by step, in due course we will achieve our destination. The thing that can most unsettle us when faced with a situation in which we feel exposed is taking our eyes off our goal and allowing our attention to focus on the present circumstances. Don't look down!

## 5. Do see the job through to completion

Transitions take much longer to complete than I had ever previously realized. And they take even longer to become embedded in the life of a church such that they become the new and accepted reality. Those of us who have an aspiration to lead change need to have a long-term perspective and to understand that our job is not done until we have seen the very culture of the church changed. I was determined not to move on from Emmanuel Church until I had seen not only the culture change but also structures established and leaders put in place who would ensure the continuance and development of this new culture well after my own leadership span had come to an end.

Probably the thing which gave me greatest satisfaction about my time in Saltburn was actually what happened after I left and moved on. The church was determined to appoint a successor to me who was thoroughly in sympathy with the new ethos of the church and someone who would own and further the values of the New Wine movement with which the church now identified. This meant that, rather than settle for any potential new minister, they were happy to wait for a suitable candidate to come along. They waited for almost two years (during which time the church actually grew!), and appointed an excellent candidate under whose ministry the church continued to flourish and to develop along the course we had set during our time there. Effective leaders of change will not be too hasty to move on and will do all that they can to ensure that the ground they have gained will not be lost but will become a springboard for future kingdom growth and development. It takes longer than we often realize!

**FURTHER READING**

William Bridges, *Managing Transitions*, London: Nicholas Brealey, 2014

Daniel Goleman, Richard Boyatzis, and Annie McKee, *Primal Leadership*, Boston, MA: Harvard Business Press, 2004

# 5

## Hosting God's Presence:
## Allowing The Spirit Freedom To Move

... the fatal mistake is to concentrate merely on the "machinery" of the church while neglecting the vitally essential work of the Holy Spirit.[1]

The greatest need of the church, and the thing which, above all others, believers ought to seek for with one mind and with their whole heart, is to be filled with the Spirit of God... Every day ought to be a Pentecostal season in the church of Christ.[2]

I am frightened by the reality that the church I lead can carry on most of our activities smoothly, efficiently, even successfully, never realising that the Holy Spirit is virtually absent from the picture. We can so easily deceive ourselves, mistaking the presence of physical bodies in a crowd for the existence of spiritual life in a community.[3]

After a couple of years in Saltburn we were encouraged by various developments. The culture of the church was steadily changing and becoming more Christ-centred and more welcoming. Worship was becoming more positive and more nourishing, we were seeing a small number of people coming to living faith in Christ, and established church members were growing in their encounter with God and in their desire to follow Him. A good number of people were positively welcoming of and enthusiastic towards the changes they were witnessing in the life of Emmanuel Church. Others tolerated what was going on, while a reasonable number of people, to be perfectly honest, absolutely hated the way the new vicar was taking "their church" (and some probably hated the new vicar into the bargain!) and were not afraid to make their feelings known. If I had compiled a list of those who were *least* in favour of what was happening in the life of Emmanuel Church, then I'm pretty sure that Carol's name would have been towards the top.

Carol had been around the church with her family for a few years prior to my arrival and led the music group which played occasionally in Sunday worship. Carol's Christian experience was entirely confined to churches of very different traditions than the one which was now emerging within Emmanuel Church and which she clearly found very threatening. This, combined with the fact that Carol had experienced significant disappointment and recent hurt in her personal life, meant that, by and large, she exercised a pretty negative influence in church meetings, and often found it hard to disguise the anger and resentment she seemed to feel towards me. Partly because she was a large personality, and partly because her husband was involved in another sphere of Christian ministry, Carol did exercise a fair bit of influence, and became something of a lightning rod for dissent and dissatisfaction within the church. I decided that the best strategy was to try to be gracious towards her, to work around her, knowing that, due to the likely trajectory of her husband's job, she wouldn't be around forever!

I recall vividly the evening Carol phoned me. The strained tone of her voice (not unfamiliar to me) had me instantly doing a mental checklist, as I tried to work out what on earth I might have done this time, and about which she was phoning to complain. I was more than taken aback when she explained that she was actually phoning to inform me that her husband had, completely out of the blue, left her for someone else. I spent the rest of the evening with Carol and her family in their home, sharing with them in their grief, witnessing their stunned disbelief, and, ultimately, praying with them.

Over the succeeding weeks Carol would come regularly to our home and pour out her heart to us. As she felt unable to pray herself, and lacking significant spiritual resources within herself, we would listen to her, pray for her, and then sit with her as she wept uncontrollably, often for an hour at a time. Through her brokenness, Carol was beginning to open up to God in a way she had never previously done. However, when, some few months later, she turned up for the first time at our regular midweek Open to God meeting, I am not sure that I was quite able to conceal my astonishment. I was more than a little fearful that, relatively restrained though the meeting was, she might be completely freaked by the whole experience.

Nevertheless, Carol became a regular member of that group and, though still fearful, began to make tentative steps forward in her walk with God. It was after one meeting that she followed me through to my study in order to let me know about yet another new traumatic twist in the unravelling of her marriage. It was too big to discuss there and then so I suggested I simply pray for her and that we meet at another time. I honestly felt quite unable to offer very much at all by way of help or encouragement and felt as powerless as she herself felt in the light of her circumstances. So I found myself praying over her the classic prayer of the helpless pastor – "Come Holy Spirit". As we waited and as I laid hands on Carol, I couldn't help noticing that she was remarkably still and quiet (her default mode when being prayed for was to sob uncontrollably). In those days, I still used to pray with my eyes closed,[4] so I half opened one to see what was happening. Carol was sprawled over the armchair in which she was sitting, apparently unconscious, and very evidently under the power of the Holy Spirit. I did the only thing I could think of – I prayed "More, Lord", and went to get my wife Nadine! For two hours we prayed over Carol, blessing what God was doing, affirming the presence of the Spirit, and watching Carol alternately weep and laugh uproariously, as God did a major work of restoration and healing. It was simply glorious.

When she finally came round and staggered to her feet, she did so as a completely different person. A friend bumping into her in town a couple of days later, seeing the profound transformation and what can only be described as the glory of the Lord upon her, demanded to know what on earth had happened to her! When Carol explained that the vicar had prayed for her, the friend asked if the vicar might pray for her too!

The inward transformation that God brought about within Carol resulted in a whole new attitude, a deep love for God and for His presence, and became outwardly visible in a new radiance. Carol became a wonderfully anointed worship leader with a profound sensitivity to the Spirit of God (there were times when, in the middle of worship/ministry times, as the piano playing became a little "slurred", we had to go over and gently help Carol off the piano stool and lay her out on the floor as the Holy Spirit overwhelmed her!). Carol ultimately became one of our key leaders, a very dear personal friend, and, much to the dismay of her former associates, one of the greatest champions of the kingdom transformations we were seeking to see brought about in the life of the church.

I suppose I learned two key lessons through this time.

Firstly, God is well able to change even the hardest people and overturn the most determined opposition. Indeed, while I have, subsequently, still prayed that God might move certain people on from our church, I have realized that His preferred way of operating is to change people and to get them onside with His purposes. Seeing people not as they currently are, or as they present themselves, but rather as whom they might become through the work of Christ, is actually a far more helpful and hopeful way of operating. I guess that this is what the apostle Paul is describing when he writes, "we have stopped evaluating people from a human point of view".[5]

Secondly, and more significantly, I learned in a very practical way the imperative for all leaders of creating within a local church a climate where the Holy Spirit is free to act and in which people are encouraged and enabled to experience His fullness and empowering presence. I discovered that what I was still struggling to see happen after many months of trying, the Holy Spirit was sometimes able to bring about in minutes if allowed to do so. The realization dawned on me then that, if we have any aspiration to see kingdom transformation come to our own church, and if we want to see people changed, then whatever else we do, our top priority needs to be that of making space for the work of the Holy Spirit. Ultimately, He is the only one who can bring genuine and lasting change to any church and its people. We need to take positive steps to welcome Him among us.

## DON'T TRY THIS ON YOUR OWN

The Bible, and the history of God's dealings with His people, is full of warnings about the futility of trying to do the work of God in our own human strength and by virtue of our own unaided efforts. When God speaks to the Jewish leader

Zerubbabel about the great work of Temple rebuilding God has called him to oversee, He reminds him that this work cannot be achieved by *might* (human prowess or ability) nor by *power* (physical strength or natural resources), but only by the Spirit of God.[6] Jesus himself, after giving careful instructions to His first disciples concerning the continuance of His ministry in the era following His return to the Father, warns them not to even contemplate setting out on this great adventure until they have received the Father's promise of the infilling with the Spirit.[7] As Brad Long puts it:

> *The need to be baptised with the Holy Spirit is so vital that Jesus confined his disciples to Jerusalem until they had received this gift. Their mission field was the world, and they faced determined opposition from the same forces that had murdered Jesus. Taking the gospel to the world was a daunting, seemingly impossible task, and God's agenda for the believers was one of prayerful waiting rather than zealous working. The time for work would come, but first they needed to receive the spiritual equipping that would see them and future generations all doing the same thing that Jesus himself had done – calling people into God's Kingdom, driving out the forces of evil, bringing hope and healing, and witnessing the manifest presence of God in the midst of mundane life. It is foolish and usually disastrous for untrained, unequipped soldiers to be sent into battle. It is equally foolish for the church to commission its missionaries or to ordain its pastors and elders without first ensuring that they receive the full equipping that Jesus said they would need.[8]*

We need to be clear as to what Jesus means by His injunction not to "get ahead" of the work of the Spirit. He is not in any way advocating a form of spiritual passivity. Sometimes it is possible to fall into the trap of assuming that the work of the Spirit is so entirely distinct from our own spheres of work for God that there is really very little, if any, overlap. He has His work to do, and we have ours. Might I suggest that such an attitude is something of an abdication of our proper responsibility? What God is looking for, Scripture seems to suggest, is a *partnership* with those who belong to Him, in which He undertakes to equip us for the specific enterprises in which He has called us to engage.

The trouble is, most of us find it very hard to inhabit the reality of such a partnership. We have little difficulty doing things *for* God, operating as if God had told us that He was now weary after all His historic activity on earth and was going to have an extended rest while we got on with things. Equally, we are often comfortable with the idea that some things are best left entirely up to God and to the exercise of His sovereign will, while we just observe from a distance without getting involved. It is the working together with Him, under His direction and in the power of His Spirit (and with all the uncertainty that this entails) that we find rather hard to navigate. Yet this is exactly the nature of life in the Spirit, of life in God's kingdom, which the Scriptures present as normal.

My own story, not unlike that of many others, is one of having to learn the hard way that the key to real fruitfulness is solely to be found through an openness to and a partnership with the Holy Spirit. I found myself in local church leadership in my mid-twenties, and probably felt I had a good deal to prove to myself, to others, and to God. I was regarded as naturally gifted in a number of key areas and was happy to put those gifts to good use in the cause of God's kingdom. On the surface I must have appeared fairly competent and effective but, to be honest, much of the time I felt like someone out of their depth and battling against strong currents which threatened to overwhelm me. Strong swimmers who find themselves in such situations are the last people to accept help or even to see their need for help. It is those who come to the end of their own resources and sense themselves to be drowning who will trust themselves to another.

It took several years for me to come to the end of my own resources, and it happened in a pretty dramatic way as I found myself completely out of my depth in a ministry situation and plunged into bitter depression. God allowed me to go through several months of what I can only describe as a wilderness experience – months in which I cried out more and more desperately to Him for help and in which I came progressively to the end of any confidence I had in my own ability to accomplish anything for Him. It was the most painful time of my life, a time of the most profound emptying. But the fruit of it was truly glorious because it led me to understand completely that I had no hope but God, no capacity to accomplish anything other than that which He might do through me; that real fruitfulness lay in complete reliance on the presence and power of the Holy Spirit. It happened to coincide with my being appointed as vicar of Emmanuel Church.

## FOLLOWING THE EXAMPLE OF JESUS

This should not surprise us in that this, if you like, is the paradigm of kingdom life and service which Jesus Himself, the prototype Spirit-filled human being, lives out and models for us. Jesus, unlike us, actually did possess "natural" or innate powers and abilities which could have accomplished a great deal on earth. But in order to fulfil His own unique calling and in order to model for us the dynamics of the Spirit-filled life, in coming to earth He laid aside everything that put Him at an advantage over us. This is exactly what the apostle Paul is writing about in Philippians 2:6ff and what the writer of the epistle to the Hebrews is describing when he refers to the need for Jesus to become "like his brethren in all things".[9] He lays aside His own heavenly powers and authority and empties Himself, thus putting Himself in a position where He is now open to receive the infilling and equipping of the Spirit of God. The narratives of Jesus' baptism[10] describe this dramatic infilling and mark the beginning of Jesus' ministry of proclaiming the presence of God's kingdom rule in a definitive way on earth. He, Himself, is true to the injunction He will subsequently give to His first disciples; He refuses to embark upon ministry before He has been properly equipped by the Father.

Throughout Jesus' ministry we see and hear echoes of this kingdom dynamic of emptying and receiving the fullness of the Spirit. When faced with the challenges and disrespect of the religious authorities who assert that His power to set the demonized free must come from the devil, Jesus instead insists that it is the Spirit of God working through Him[11] that has caused this (as opposed to any power inherent in Himself). He is always on the lookout to see what the Father is doing and determined at all times to work in partnership with Him.[12] Little wonder that there is such a contrast observed between the ministry of Jesus and both that of other contemporary religious leaders who have to rely purely on their own resources[13] and that of even His own disciples who have yet to experience the Spirit's anointing.[14]

It must have been the experience of three years observing the way in which Jesus operated which shaped the convictions and praxis of those same disciples as they engaged in kingdom ministry in the period following Pentecost. The way they pray at a time when under threat of serious opposition[15] gives us a helpful insight into their modus operandi. They fully appreciate that they have responsibilities to fulfil, specifically those of making known as widely as possible the good news of the kingdom of God. For this they will need God to strengthen and equip them and to give them boldness. Their prayer is not simply for such boldness, however; it is also a request that God might stretch out His hand to heal and to perform the signs and wonders associated with the presence of His kingdom. Their prayer for this might well be summarized by simply praying, "Come, Holy Spirit".

If we want to see the kingdom come fully in the churches in whose leadership we share, or of which we are members – if we want to see lives and attitudes changed – then we need to pray like those first disciples did. Of course we will ask for God's help in the specific works He has called us to undertake and especially for boldness in bearing witness to Him. But we will also need repeatedly to invite Him to make His powerful presence known in sovereign ways. We will need to welcome His Spirit and give Him space to work among us. How might we begin to do this, and what might it look like?

## OPENING THE DOOR

Possibly the biggest culture change we might be required to bring about in most churches, and the one which is probably key to everything else changing, is to do with people's expectancy when it comes to personal spiritual experience. The idea that God might be present to us in a way which makes a difference is not one, sadly, that a large number of worshippers readily entertain. I say this without any shred of blame; they simply have never been encouraged to cultivate such an expectation and probably have been immersed in a church culture in which such expectation would never be raised. A door needs to be opened for people into a fuller and more direct experience of God. An expectation needs to be raised that there is more on offer than we have thus far experienced and a hunger stirred for a deeper encounter with God and with the fullness of His Spirit. The role of leaders is critical in opening up this door and encouraging others to walk through it.

An obvious place to start with this is in the regular week by week Sunday preaching. Preaching feeds into the life of a local church in all manner of ways. One of its key impacts, however, is to shape the culture of the church and to help people form a backdrop against which they can faithfully act out their own lives. By rehearsing the story of God and His people, especially those dimensions of the story of which they have thus far been unaware, we are inviting people to step out in new ways and undertake new adventures in their walk with God. People always respond more easily to narrative as opposed to more conceptual teaching, so it's probably most helpful to begin with a series of sermons, for example, on people whom Jesus met. This gives us an opportunity to look at the impact Jesus had upon those people, how their lives were changed, and thus what we might reasonably expect Jesus to do in our own lives today.

A series on the life of the early church in the opening chapters of the Acts of the Apostles might be a good follow-up as we explore, not only the nature of the church that God has in mind, but also what clues these chapters give us as to how we might expect to see God at work among us today. Only then, after we have considered some real-life experiences together, might it be time to explore a more systematic theology of the person and work of the Holy Spirit. To this end, we could look at Old Testament prophecy, and the teaching of Jesus and Paul surrounding his ministry in the church and the world.

Learning, of course, consists of far more than simply being taught. People usually need a context in which they can process (especially unfamiliar) teaching with others. I have already touched upon "Open to God", the weekly meeting that I launched shortly after becoming vicar of Saltburn. It was designed to be a place where, in due course, people might encounter the presence of God in a more immediate way, and one of the central constituent parts to each evening was engaging together with Scripture. People were able to articulate concerns and doubts, as well as describe their own growing sense of encounter with God. They gradually began to inhabit the biblical narrative in a wholly different way. The process of learning and sharing together (a very new thing) meant that this story became a shared story and people began to have a sense of being on a common journey.

Bringing in others to teach and to reinforce our own teaching is usually a fruitful strategy. All of us who are church leaders will have had the simultaneously encouraging yet frustrating experience of having church members respond to the ministry of visiting preachers who have said nothing different from what we ourselves have taught, yet with no obvious impact! Perhaps it is simply having the message reinforced, or hearing it with fresh ears from a fresh voice, that makes the difference.

........................................
## MODELLING

*Leaders mould congregations. The leader's task is to so shape the culture and ethos of the church that it becomes a context in which the dynamic of cooperating with the Holy Spirit of God may take place. Leaders must therefore be living models of what it means to follow Jesus Christ, for only then can they shape the congregation into a dynamic expression of the Kingdom of God.*[16]

It is one thing to talk and teach about the work of the Spirit. However, many people will only readily open up to the possibility of embracing new reality when they see it demonstrated. As we have already observed, cultural change can never be dictated but has to be commended and demonstrated. Simon Western, in his fresh and insightful work *Leadership*, describes leaders as "cultural avatars... Acting on behalf of cultures that animate them as leaders, they become skilled transmitters of the cultures in which they swim."[17] If we want to see people live more naturally in the realm of the Spirit, then we need to model what this kind of living actually looks like and consciously represent a spiritual culture that might be completely unknown to those whom we serve. In personal, everyday, one-to-one ministry with those whom we meet we can raise expectations in the ways in which we pray for them. Consciously seeking to listen out for what God might be saying when we pray with or counsel people, and then having the courage to offer such prophetic words, raises people's faith and expectancy. As people – like Carol, whom we met earlier – experience the healing presence of God and tell their stories to others, so others begin to grow in expectation that they too might experience something similar.

I firmly believe that those entrusted with leadership responsibility have a unique capacity either to open or close the door to the work of the Holy Spirit in the life of a local church. I have met numbers of such leaders who warm to the idea, in theory, of God working powerfully in their own church, who even relish experiencing the powerful work of God in their own lives, but who find themselves unable to release this in the life of their church. It usually boils down to an issue of courage, a fear of going out on a limb. My experience is that unless and until we are prepared to stick our necks out for the sake of God's work then we will remain disappointed with what we see taking place.

I started out in my ministry in Saltburn longing for people to come into a full experience of the Spirit's presence and life. To be perfectly honest, for the first two years of my time there, I was rather hoping that this might take place in a manner that would cause as little disruption and mess as possible! It wasn't just that I was concerned about losing face myself; I honestly wanted to protect God's reputation and to make sure that people were not put off the business of pressing on with Him because of the untidy ways in which He might act! I do find it astonishing, and rather presumptuous, the way in which we fall into the temptation of trying to protect God's reputation and to stop Him from doing things others might find difficult.

Of course such a tendency is the exact opposite of that which we are advocating in this chapter. If we want to see God move in power then we have to surrender control and give Him space to move as He determines. I still remember very clearly talking to God about this, and well recall the evening when I acknowledged to Him that Emmanuel was His church, and not mine, and that whatever He wanted to do was just fine by me. I remember immediately experiencing a fresh infilling with God's Spirit as I prayed and, looking back, can easily see this as the springboard for a season of much greater Holy Spirit activity within the church and community. I found that the determination to welcome God's Spirit was not a one-off thing but a decision which I had to take repeatedly. I found it helpful, in those days, to lock myself in the church building for half an hour every Saturday evening, to pray around the building, to worship in an unrestrained way (hence the locked doors!), and to welcome the Spirit's presence over our church and community. Little wonder that we began to see more people coming to Christ, some of our more traditional people swept off their feet by the

Holy Spirit (quite literally!), and some wonderful physical and emotional healings. When we welcome Him, He comes.

## PROVIDING OPPORTUNITY FOR ENCOUNTER

The Holy Spirit has often been described as the perfect gentleman; He only goes where He is invited. If we want to see Him work, we need to invite Him; and we are often remiss at making space for this. I wanted, from the outset of my ministry in Saltburn, to give people opportunity for direct encounter with God and realized that, at least in the early stages, the rather formal Sunday worship was probably not going to be the place where this would most easily happen. Open to God was designed to be a place where worship, teaching, and ministry could take place in the relaxed atmosphere of a home and where people could explore spiritual things in a fresh way. It proved to be the engine that drove the renewal of the whole church.

Many people fear that a new minister coming in to a church is going to stop or change their most cherished activities (usually the ways in which they have become accustomed to worshipping on Sundays). It is entirely possible to start something new that will significantly move forward the spiritual life of the church without offending anyone by messing with that which is most dear to them. Of course, as people grow in their experience of God and their excitement at meeting with Him, then they will provide the impetus for seeing change come about in other aspects of church life.

John Wimber often used to say, "If you want to get wet, then go where the rain is falling." Not only is it good to introduce people to experiences elsewhere that will move them forward in their walk with God, but there is something about going out of our own familiar context for opening us up much more to receiving from God in a new way. In our early years in Saltburn we managed to persuade a good number of church members to spend a church weekend away together each year. I took the opportunity to invite trusted friends to come to speak and lead ministry, and for many of our church members these were times when they first began to experience something more of God's power and presence.

It was for exactly this reason – a desire to provide a context in which people could experience kingdom ministry at first hand and be trained in it – that the New Wine Movement was founded in 1989 by David Pytches (then vicar of St Andrew's Chorleywood). Having been significantly impacted by the ministry of John Wimber and having mentored numbers of local church leaders in kingdom ministry, David was prevailed upon by those very leaders to find a way of helping them induct their own church members into this ministry. He hit upon the notion of a summer holiday conference where local churches could camp together, thus building their common life, and where people could gain a vision for church in the power of the Spirit and then go home with the determination to see such a vision fulfilled in their own places. It has proved, over more than twenty-five years, to be a wonderfully effective model.[18] For us in Saltburn, taking people off to the New Wine summer conferences was easily one of the most significant factors in the development of the life of our own church (as it was, equally, some years later when we moved to our current church), if for no other reason than that it convinced our church members that their vicar was not the only nutcase on the planet!

A full week's experience of immersion in the ministry of the Holy Spirit can have a profound impact upon individuals and churches. Over the years, it has been thrilling to see broken lives healed as people, over a period of days, go deeper into the presence of God. It has been wonderful to see people catch a vision for serving God in new and exciting ways and being supernaturally equipped for such ministries. It has been a joy to see the supernatural ministry of the Spirit become the most normal thing in the world for children and young people and their own vision for serving God develop and grow through encounter with Him. It has been a profound relief to see people gaining a richer and fuller understanding of what our own church might become and what place it might have in the life of our community. In the hothouse environment of a summer conference people have opportunity to make rapid growth. Such people become one's key advocates for kingdom change and development back home. Taking them to summer conferences[19] might just be the most useful thing you ever do if you want to see things move forward in your own church.

## BRINGING IT INTO THE CENTRE

A few years ago, a newly converted member of our church had brought a friend to our evening service for the very first time. The service had clearly gone on a bit longer than the friend had bargained for, and when I had finished preaching and invited people to stand, as we always do, in order to welcome the ministry of the Spirit, the visitor made to leave quietly. Her friend grabbed her arm to stop her leaving. "Don't go just yet," I heard her whisper. "This is the best bit!"

Without entering into any discussion of what is the relative importance of worship and teaching and any other components of public worship, for this woman, one thing was already pretty clear to her. You were cheating people if you didn't give them opportunity to encounter God's presence in a direct and straightforward way.

I don't much care how this ministry is carried out and organized in Sunday worship, but I do care that it is done.

I fully appreciate the time constraints upon us (especially on busy Sunday mornings) and all that has to be fitted into our gatherings for worship. But my feeling is that all of us make time and space for what we deem to be most important. Too many services (especially, in my experience, Anglican ones!) are honestly too cluttered. I appreciate the structure of Anglican worship (the tradition in which I have been formed), with its emphasis on ensuring that we keep the right elements at the heart of worship (ministry of the word, intercession, confession of sin with the declaration of forgiveness, affirmation of faith, and so on). I appreciate many of the words we habitually use in worship; I just think we use far too many most of the time and that "less is more". Most of us need to get into the habit of saying a little bit less to God, and giving Him greater space to minister more directly to us.

The obvious place to incorporate this into the flow of public worship is probably at the end of the sermon, when it becomes something of a way of facilitating a response to what has been preached. We have heard (hopefully!) God speak to us through His word. Now we are asking Him to "enact" His word in our lives and bring about the reality of what we have had explained to us. Our practice is to invite people to stand, and I usually invite people to extend their hands as if to receive a gift. Posture is important, and both standing and extending our hands signify that we want to engage with God and to receive from Him.

I may well begin by giving people space to own before God the specific things on their hearts as a result of God having spoken to them, even encouraging them to articulate to Him what it is that they most want Him to do in them and for them. I will then very simply pray "Come Holy Spirit". I find it important, from time to time, to remind people that this is not something the leader or minister is "doing to them". Neither I, nor anyone else, has the capacity to "summon up" the Spirit of God. Rather, I am praying on behalf of all of us and encouraging everyone present to pray similarly and to welcome, in their own way, the presence of God. Of course, it is not that He is not present until we invite Him. Rather, we are acknowledging that He is always present, but asking Him now to enable us to recognize and welcome His presence, cooperating with Him in whatever it is that He wants to do among us.

Then, we wait, and don't feel obliged to fill the silence. Ministry of this nature is not filling all the space with spoken words. It really is waiting, and consciously focusing on the presence of God among us. We are sometimes embarrassed by silence and sometimes fearful of it. Too often we feel that we have to fill it, as if by doing so we might make something happen for people. But waiting, gently encouraging people to press into God's presence, and trusting that He is encountering people in the stillness, is a necessary discipline for us. It only needs to be for five minutes or so, but we must never underestimate the impact that such ministry repeatedly practised can have on the life of a church. People begin to be changed by God and to experience His healing presence. People grow in their own expectancy towards Him and begin to integrate the discipline of waiting on God into their own personal devotional lives. People come to worship, week by week, with a greater sense of expectancy and excitement; and those who come as seekers are struck by the fact that God is not simply spoken about but actually seems to be at work here.

It is helpful to offer more intentional personal prayer ministry for those who might value it, and to have a trained and trusted team of people to draw alongside and either bless what God is doing or, in the case of those who find it more difficult to sense God's closeness, to help them press into His presence. We do this in a variety of ways. Often the biggest constraint is the layout of the building. Sometimes we invite people to step out into the aisles of the building as a sign of wanting to step out and step up with God. If the ministry time is taking place in the middle, as opposed to at the end of, a service, I will often invite people who would value personal prayer ministry to go to the lounge area at the back of church where ministry can go on simultaneously with the rest of the service. Especially when people are reluctant to move out of their places, I have often invited those who would like prayer simply to remain in their places at the end of the service while the ministry team come round to lay hands on them and to bless them. This is a really helpful way of starting out in getting prayer ministry established in the culture of Sunday worship. Sometimes, especially in some evening services (when time seems less of a pressure), we have simply had extended times of worship when people have been invited to find a space within the building and "soak" in the presence of God.

Finally, if you want to encourage an openness to the ministry of the Spirit, give space in public worship and at other times to tell stories of what God is doing. There is something very powerful about testimony; it raises expectation and arouses hunger in others for more of God. What we celebrate, that we propagate.

"Come, Holy Spirit!"

....................................................................

**FURTHER READING AND RESOURCES**

Gary Best, *Naturally Supernatural*, Cape Town: Vineyard International, 2008

Bill Johnson, *Face to Face with God*, Lake Mary, FL: Charisma House, 2007

Simon Ponsonby, *More*, Eastbourne: Kingsway, 2004

John Wimber, *Power Evangelism*, Sevenoaks: Hodder and Stoughton, 1985

New Wine offer a range of training days and similar resources designed to help local churches grow in their experience of the ministry of the Spirit. There are day conferences on such topics as:

- *learning to heal*
- *developing pastoral prayer in the local church*
- *growing in the prophetic*
- *spiritual gifts for all*

These are run regularly by trained practitioners in local New Wine Network churches, and video and other resources are available for such events to be run on a more ad hoc basis by local churches and small groups. More details of these, and other resources, can be found at www.new-wine.org.

# 6

## Increasing Capacity:
## Growing And Developing Leaders

Leadership should be empowering. It is the process of giving power away, not collecting it. It is moving the power to influence into the hands of the people we are leading so that they can pursue the mission. Leadership exists to serve the mission and to serve the people. Like God's leadership, leadership is a relationship that cares enough to walk patiently with people towards a shared purpose. It is not about leaders; it is about the people we lead.[1]

All effective leaders can point to someone who encouraged them and gave time and energy to develop them, and trusted them with responsibility.[2]

The clergy–laity dichotomy... is one of the principal obstacles to the church effectively being God's agent of the Kingdom today because it creates a false idea that only "holy men", namely ordained ministers, are really qualified and responsible for leadership and significant ministry.[3]

Imagine your house is on fire and the blaze is threatening to get out of control. You are standing in front of it with a bucket of water in your hand. On the ground next to you are twelve sleeping firemen. Here's the question: where do you throw the water?

The knee-jerk reaction for many leaders is to throw the water on the fire. Of course, at one level, we have a deep-seated feeling that one bucket may not do a huge amount of good given the size of the fire. But the sheer scale and urgency of the task drives us to want to do something to make a difference, and one bucketful is better than no water at all. You never know what impact it might have. And if others follow our example then we might just damp down the blaze.

The task facing us in turning round the culture of a local church may well feel quite similar in nature and scale to that of overcoming a blazing fire. There are two traps we are most prone to falling into in tackling it, both in different ways akin to throwing our bucket of water on the fire (as opposed to on the firemen!). We can focus on changing structures and mechanisms rather than people (we can become too task focused). Alternatively, we can take too much responsibility upon ourselves and try to go it alone, rather than standing back from the blaze and recruiting others with whom we might share the task and whose contribution may likely result in the task being accomplished far more effectively and efficiently.

Seeing appropriate structures established is not unimportant in effective change management, and such structures are vital for the long-term health and vitality of any church. The wrong structures can seriously hinder the church's capacity to fulfil God's calling upon it. In the next chapter we will be exploring what might be appropriate structures for facilitating the mission and growth of a church.

However, paying attention to structures will achieve nothing at all if we do not pay at least as much attention to developing and investing in people. Because structures are inanimate and do not answer back, and are, therefore, easier to change than people, many leaders are drawn into investing too much time and effort in structural or organizational change and neglect the core business of seeing people developed. This is a harder business but is actually the only way to achieve organizational change. Many leaders find themselves ultimately disappointed and disillusioned (not to say exhausted) because they have tinkered with their church structures in every way imaginable. They have attended conferences and learning communities and have read the latest books on strategies for growing churches. Yet they still have not seen the results they had hoped for and still have a church full of resistant people who just do not seem to get it (and who are becoming increasingly wary of the next scheme the vicar is trying to impose upon them).

Our error may not actually lie in an over-fixation with changing structures; it may simply be that we are trying to do too much by ourselves. In the early stages of turnaround leadership, and especially when we are seeking to reshape and recalibrate most aspects of the life of the church and its ministry, we may well have to get directly involved in leading in virtually every aspect of the church's life and ministry. However, as a long-term strategy, this pace-setting style of leadership is a recipe for personal exhaustion: the scope and impact of the church's ministry will never exceed the physical and spiritual limits determined by the capabilities and capacity of the senior leader. The leader's resources will be spent long before there is any possibility of the fire being brought under control. The wisest and most effective leaders pay a good deal of attention to, and spend a good deal of their energies in, the business of raising up and investing in other leaders. As John Maxwell puts it:

*A leader is great not because of his/her power,*
*but because of their ability to empower others.*
*A worker's main responsibility is doing the work*

*himself. A leader's main responsibility is developing others to do the work.*[4]

Nehemiah arrives in Jerusalem with a massive programme to tackle. I suspect that many contemporary leaders in his position, judging by the way they go about leadership and ministry in their current contexts, would have rolled their sleeves up and started to lay bricks. Of course they would realize that they could never see the walls rebuilt in their own lifetime, but they could make a small difference on a limited scale. They could read some books on advanced bricklaying which might help them. They could even join a support group along with other city rebuilders, where they could swap notes about how hard bricklaying is today, and how few people understand the challenges facing rebuilders.

Nehemiah appears to take a completely different approach. Chapter 3 of his book details the long list of people – many of them unlikely candidates – all of whom, fired by Nehemiah's vision for a rebuilt city, set to and began to share in the work of rebuilding. Nehemiah's great strategy was to recruit and release a huge workforce who, together, accomplished a monumental rebuilding project in record time. His role was to envision them, equip them, oversee them, and encourage them.

## FOLLOWING THE EXAMPLE OF JESUS

When we look at the ministry of Jesus, it is striking to notice how He invested His own personal time and energies. Faced with the huge task of seeing the world reconciled to God, He confined himself throughout his brief ministry to a very limited geographical area. In the early years of that ministry He is recorded as preaching to large crowds and exercising a wide-ranging ministry throughout, especially, the northern part of Israel. However, as His ministry grows in focus and towards its climax in His sacrificial death and resurrection, we find Jesus spending an increasing amount of time with a small group of twelve hand-picked followers. These are those whom He has identified to be the ones to oversee the extension of His ministry beyond His own earthly career. As a preparation for this He is putting them through an intensive training experience which becomes, in many ways, His own major focus during His final months on earth.

If Jesus' greatest concern was to multiply His own ministry by raising up and equipping others, and if our own leadership and ministry is to resemble His, then we need to take much more seriously the priority of growing kingdom capacity by developing other leaders. Such investment may well be the most significant thing we do in our whole ministries. After all, Jesus' strategy has proved to be exceptionally effective. The movement which, at the end of His time on earth, numbered around 100, grew within three centuries to number more than 30 million, and today has more than 2 billion living members distributed across every continent. It continues to grow, especially in places where the church and its leaders seek faithfully to imitate the example of Jesus of investing in the few for the sake of the many. Let's take a closer look at the example Jesus sets and imagine what it might mean for us to take Him as our model in this work of developing others.

## 1. Growing disciples

We have discussed at some length the understanding that at the heart of leadership is the business of exercising influence for God. The best influencers are those who allow themselves to grow in their capacity to be influenced *by* God. Thus, leaders might well be described as *lead followers*. One of the key qualities we will look for in identifying potential leaders is that of teachability and a desire to be a lifelong learner from God and from others. So, our first step in leadership recruitment and training is to focus on growing followers of Jesus, or disciples.

At some stage in the early to middle part of His ministry, Jesus takes Himself away for a night of prayer to discuss with His Father whom to choose and appoint as His first leadership team.[5] These are chosen from a much wider pool of people who are following Jesus and who have been called to be apprentices to Him in the ministry of the kingdom.[6] The first step in this process of recruiting a leadership team was taken many months beforehand, when Jesus began to extend to a range of people an invitation to follow Him and to join his band of kingdom servants. Most of the stories we are told by the Gospel writers are of those who responded positively to this call.[7]

However, it is equally clear that not all those who were promising candidates for discipleship, and who were called by Jesus to follow Him, were able to accept the cost of such a challenge. The rich young ruler whom we meet in Mark 10 looks to have an excellent portfolio of leadership attributes and qualities, and appears to have the potential to be a superb asset to Jesus and His mission. Sadly, there is at least one major area of his life which he is unwilling to submit to the lordship of Jesus and which ultimately prevents him from being able to follow Jesus. Jesus is looking for leaders who have something of a track record in terms of a willingness to be influenced by Him and to follow Him.

Our first step in growing others is to extend a wide invitation to people to become disciples. We may find ourselves in a local church situation in which the true nature of discipleship has never properly been spelled out. How might we lay a foundation for helping people enter into and then progress on the discipleship journey?

We probably need to begin by using the opportunities afforded by Sunday preaching and teaching to paint a broad-brush picture of authentic discipleship as the Bible describes it. We will want to explore such areas as:

- Jesus' call to each one of us to follow Him in an intentional way and to be shaped by Him. Examining the experience of the first disciples and imagining ourselves in their position will be helpful in this;

- what it means to grow in a relationship with God and to love Him with all our heart, mind, soul, and strength, being shaped by encounter with Him;

- what it means to make Jesus truly Lord of our life, especially in the areas of relationships with others, attitudes to money and possessions, obedience;

- understanding our call to share in Jesus' ministry to others in the power of the Spirit;

- understanding that we have been enlisted in the mission of Jesus to make the good news of His kingdom known more widely and to help others experience His call in their own lives.

It certainly seems to be the case that Jesus begins by teaching in this way, describing the reality of life in God's kingdom such that people are equipped and inspired to reimagine their own lives in the light of this new reality.

Preaching has a vital role to play in laying down foundational teaching (which is why we need to plan carefully our teaching series for Sundays), but in and of itself it will not grow disciples. People need to have opportunity to dialogue with Scripture and to tease out its implications for their own lives. They need to have a context in which they can share their difficulties and reservations, to express doubts and find reassurance, and be prayed for as they move forward on the discipleship journey. They need a place where they can be shaped and coached by us as leaders as they take their first tentative steps forward.

I have already mentioned that the first step we took in Saltburn to foster growth in discipleship was to start a weekly midweek meeting in our home. As the group grew, so we transitioned into a number of much smaller and more intimate "lifegroups", of between six and twelve people, with a clear focus on helping one another grow in missional discipleship. We'll have more to say about healthy small groups in the next chapter. It is sufficient for now simply to say that these are the basic building blocks of any church which is going to take seriously the business of growing disciples.

One of the most important aspects of growing disciples is that of envisioning people for what they might become under the influence of Jesus. When Jesus calls His first disciples, explicit in the call is a promise that He will make them what they never could be without His help, and that they will find themselves serving way beyond their natural abilities and capacity.[8] We need to foster similar hope in the hearts of those whom we are called to lead and to disciple. We need not only in our own minds to see everyone as a potential leader, but we also need to encourage others to set their sights high in terms of how God might use them. One of the prayers I often find myself praying is that God would use me to raise up leaders who will outstrip me in every way. When we have this kind of growth mindset, and when we encourage it in others, then there is no limit to how far those whom we are developing might progress.

## 2. Identifying potential leaders

The best potential leaders tend to be people who do not push themselves forward, but rather are those who, like cream, simply rise to the surface. What are the particular qualities we ought to look for and which identify people as having leadership potential?

## Christlike character

Some years ago, when praying about who might be the next group of leaders to develop in our church, I sensed the Lord asking me a question. "Who," He seemed to be asking, "are the people about whom you would say, 'I wish I had a church full of people like them'? Those are the ones you should be raising up." I suppose He was essentially asking me what kind of influence I wanted to see exercised through the life of our church. Thus the people I am always trying to identify are those who aspire to imitate Christ and who strive to grow in their resemblance to His character.

The New Testament constantly stresses character and personal holiness over giftedness or anointing when it describes the attributes of an effective leader.[9] Those who have spent any time in developing others know full well that it is much easier to train and equip a person of character in ministry skills than it is to instil character into a supremely talented person. Few leaders and ministers come off the rails due to a lack of giftedness, but all too many do because of character flaws and moral weaknesses. As the great nineteenth-century Scottish preacher Robert Murray McCheyne observed in his journal, "It is not great talents God blesses so much as great likeness to Jesus. A holy minister is an awful weapon in the hands of God!"[10]

In particular, I am looking for people who are servant-hearted, who conduct themselves with humility and grace, and who demonstrate a clear intention to follow Christ, with a clear determination to order their lives according to a biblical understanding of holiness. These people will always exercise influence, as Walter Wright observes:

*Character is life lived in relationship with God; it is about being the person God intends you to be for the sake of the people whom God brings across your path. People of character become leaders whether they hold a position of leadership or not.*[11]

## Love for people

Leadership is fundamentally about people rather than about position or task. Thus the most promising potential leaders are those who love people and have a commitment to serving them and helping them grow. A friend of mine suggests that one of the best places to identify potential new leaders is during coffee after Sunday worship. He tells me that he tries to identify both those to whom others are drawn, and those who go looking for other people, especially those who are either new to the church or who are by themselves. Those who show an interest in and concern for others are very likely those who will be most effective in leading others well.

## Positive mindset

Leaders are called to deal in hope, to stimulate the exercise of faith, and to focus people on the hope we have in Christ. They are called to encourage and to build others up, bringing the best out of those whom they lead. Leaders are responsible for shaping and defining the atmosphere in the sphere over which they have responsibility. This is why churches, small groups, and other ministry areas will always to a significant extent reflect the character and personality of their leader. Leaders with a positive and faith-filled mindset bring joy and refreshment to others with whom they serve and make an invaluable contribution to any team of which they are a part. By contrast, leaders who tend to have a negative outlook can sap the energy from a team or group, dampening faith and expectancy and inhibiting the forward movement of any ministry.

A positive mindset is not an escapist or an unrealistic mindset. Nehemiah stirred up hope in those whom he was called to lead because he was able to be entirely realistic about the mess of the present situation,[12] while simultaneously pointing forward to the possibilities open to those who trust God.[13] We are looking for people who – despite present circumstances and the at times apparently overwhelming challenges of ministry – are able to inspire others to attempt great things for God.

## Spiritual gifts

It was very early on in our time in our current church. Desperate to see a properly trained and equipped healing ministry team come into being, I had invited some friends to deliver some training for us in this area. Towards the end of the afternoon, as we launched into a ministry session and encouraged people to welcome God's presence, I began to go round and lay hands on people. As I came to one particular lady I saw that her hands were literally dripping with what appeared to be oil. She herself was overwhelmed by the sense of God's Spirit resting on her and equipping her for healing ministry. Although, up to that point, she had not been especially involved in praying for others, it seemed that God was anointing her in this way. So, I began to look for every opportunity to use her (as did she!). For the last twelve years she has been most effectively used by God in ministering physical and emotional healing to others, and today, in her early eighties, she heads up our Healing on the Streets[14] team!

Not every instance of God giving gifts to people is quite so obviously and physically recognizable. However, as we look out for areas in which people are beginning to show unusual or unnatural fruitfulness, confidence, or passion, we may well begin to identify ways in which God is giving spiritual gifts to them. The best way of testing and growing such gifts is to get people involved in ministries in which those gifts can be put to good use. And the best people to allocate to specific ministry areas are those who appear to be being gifted by God for such ministries!

## Teachable spirit

Bennis and Nanus observe, on the basis of their extensive research of the practices of successful leaders, that all fruitful leaders are lifelong learners:

> *Learning is the essential fuel for the leader, the source of high octane energy that keeps up the momentum by continually sparking new understanding, new ideas and new challenges. Very simply, those who do not learn do not long survive as leaders.*[15]

We are looking for those who do not believe that they already have all the answers they need and who understand that the whole of life can be an adventure in growing in our knowledge of Jesus and in our experience of His anointing and equipping. Often it is the case that an appetite for learning and for personal growth goes hand in hand with an equal appetite to help others learn and grow. These are the kind of people the apostle Paul has in mind when he encourages Timothy to invest in faithful people who will be able to take what they have received and pass it on to others.[16]

There are some danger signs to watch out for in people which might make us circumspect in putting them in leadership positions. In many ways they are the exact opposite of the positive traits outlined above. We will steer clear of those who have manifest character flaws that they are unwilling to address, those who seem to be lacking in people skills or who come across as somewhat impatient, those whose negative outlook impacts upon them and upon others, and those who are resistant to being shaped and developed.

In addition, I have always been wary of those who seem to crave position or who are desperate to have profile and push themselves forward in some way. One tactic I have always found to be useful when someone appears to me to be angling for some role (often someone joining us from another church who wants me to know just how many areas of high-profile ministry they performed in their last church) is to thank them for their willingness to serve and then to explain where we have particular pressing needs at the moment. This may well include the coffee rota, the stewarding team, or one of the other vital teams that operates in the background. It's a good test of whether or not people are prepared to serve or simply want profile. Erwin McManus issues a stark warning to us:

> *When you lust for power you are its slave. When you live for others you are a powerful servant of God. Only those who would live to serve can be trusted with the power of God. We seem to reverse this. We pray for God's power while we contemplate whether we will choose to serve God with our lives. But the power of God without the heart of God would result in unimaginable godlessness. God finds pleasure in entrusting His power to those who are serving him in their weakness. When you pursue power and prestige, you cease to pursue character. If your ambition is to be great in the sight of men, you are not pursuing greatness in the sight of God. Some things when pulled in combination will stop you in your tracks.*[17]

I am also wary of those who want to get involved in some form of ministry in a church group as a way of excusing themselves from mission and ministry to their peers. It is always much easier helping in ministry to children or young people than it is to give ourselves to trying to reach our neighbours or those whom we meet in our life places day by day. I want to give position to and develop those who are clearly already demonstrating a desire to exercise kingdom influence in the cut and thrust of everyday life.

It has to be said that while we must never set people up to fail and ask them to take on levels of responsibility way beyond their levels of personal or spiritual maturity, I am a firm believer in getting people involved in ministry at an early stage in their Christian growth. The people who have probably grown most healthily in our own church in recent years have been those who have been encouraged to get stuck into serving from the very beginning of their Christian journey. It is for this very reason that we have trained and released numbers of our children (from age seven upwards) to be members of various ministry teams, including prayer ministry, to work alongside older and more experienced team members.

Over the years, I have been let down at times by some in whom I have placed trust and to whom I have given opportunity to serve; sometimes my "gambles" with people have not paid off. Nevertheless, I would still rather take some risks in giving opportunity to people who are relatively new in the faith, than hold people back for so long that any expectation that God might use them withers and dies before it has a chance to be tested. Dale Carnegie once pithily observed about the messiness of leadership development, "People are developed in the same way that gold is mined. Several tons of dirt must be moved to get an ounce of gold. But you don't go into the mine looking for dirt!"

We need to train ourselves to be able to spot the gold even in the most unlikely places and then work to uncover it. This is surely exactly what we see Jesus doing in inviting a group of people, who seem to be lacking in most of the expected qualifications for leadership, to follow Him and ultimately to be shaped to take responsibility for the development of His ministry.

## 3. Developing leaders

### *Providing opportunities to have a go*

The best way both of helping people gain an appetite for ministry and discerning the presence of leadership gifts or potential is to give them an opportunity to try out in some one-off or short-term area of service. We have invited those whom we suspect may have an aptitude to teach to do a short (three-minute) "call to worship" talk at the beginning of our evening services. Even if the talk bombs nothing very much is lost, but you may gain a potential preacher, and the person giving the talk gains experience in relying on God! Asking people to co-host an Alpha discussion group with you or with another experienced leader, or inviting them to shadow one of the Healing on the Streets teams for a week or two, or simply creating one-off opportunities for people to serve are all good ideas.

In my first few weeks in Saltburn I began to plan a Parish Mission for two years hence. I sold the idea as part of the church's 125th anniversary celebrations, and I certainly wasn't averse to bringing a few friends in for the week in order to help us engage in some more intentional outreach to the community. However, the principal reason behind planning that particular event was to provide an opportunity for people in the church to exercise their ministry muscles and to have a go, in a reasonably defined, short-term way, at some new ways of serving.

Jesus begins by modelling leadership and ministry to His new followers. They watch Him preaching and healing the sick and clearly develop an enthusiasm for this work.[18] Before long He is taking some of them along with Him to share in this work.[19] Eventually, and probably long before they might have thought that they were ready, Jesus pushes His twelve closest followers right out of their comfort zone and sends them out, on a short-term project, to do exactly the same things they have seen Him do.[20]

## Shaping and growing

It is not enough simply to let people have a go at ministry. They will only grow in their areas of gifting if we pay time and attention to nurturing and shaping them. Immediately after the first recorded mission of the twelve, Jesus takes them away to reflect on what has happened, to share their encouragements, and, no doubt, to process what could have gone better.[21] No one grows and develops without proper feedback.[22] It is one of our key responsibilities as leaders to ensure that we pay proper attention and give appropriate time to investing in emerging leaders in this very intentional way. I am so grateful to those who, along the way, have given me (sometimes uncomfortable but always constructive) feedback on different aspects of my own leadership and ministry. At times when I have wanted to grow in some specific aspect of my leadership, I have actively sought out someone else and asked them to coach or mentor me for a fixed period of time in that precise area, or asked for their feedback on my performance as a leader.

We learn a huge amount from the relationship the apostle Paul enjoys, especially with his own mentor Barnabas and later with his protégé Timothy. Had it not been for Barnabas, we may not have heard half so much about Paul. It was Barnabas who "took hold of him"[23] shortly after his conversion and who then introduced him to the Jerusalem church leaders. Later on, when he gets involved in the first significant church planted among those of Gentile origin, Barnabas travels some distance to seek out Saul, from the obscurity of a backwoods corner of the Roman empire, and to bring him to work alongside him in a ministry for which Barnabas believes Saul may well be especially called and equipped.[24]

I am always on the lookout for opportunities to share ministry with those I am seeking to develop. I have, on a number of occasions, "tag" preached with a younger or emerging preacher. We have spent time preparing a sermon together, doing our own independent study and waiting on God, and then coming together to pool our insights. We will then structure the sermon together. Usually I will undertake to preach the first and final sections while my protégé takes care of the middle section. We write our own sections but offer reflections to one another on our final preparation. We then preach it as a tag team. I find it a really effective way of growing people in this ministry. The point is this: all of us can find interesting and creative ways to share ministry with others in a safe and upbuilding fashion, and then work with them such that they are enabled to grow and to enjoy a real sense of sharing with us in ministry.

Ultimately, Paul rises to far greater prominence than Barnabas (whose delightful nickname literally means "son of encouragement") and outstrips his mentor. Perhaps it is Barnabas' painstaking care and attention that leaves so lasting an impression upon Paul that he, in his turn, gives himself so wholeheartedly to investing in others in order to reproduce his ministry in and through them. In his correspondence with Timothy, who has previously accompanied Paul on some of his ministry trips, we see Paul affirming and encouraging Timothy in the work God has done in him.[25] But he also gives him encouragement and exhortation in specific areas of ministry and responsibility, coaching him through some of the challenging situations which face him.[26]

## Providing resources

The most valuable resource you can give an emerging leader is your own time and attention. However, there are other practical ways in which leadership can be grown and a leadership culture established.

Early on in my time in my current church, I devised a leadership course for existing and emerging leaders. We have subsequently run this most years and continued to develop it to meet our specific training needs. It has a number of aims. We want to equip existing leaders by enlarging their vision for what God has called them into and by helping them grow, especially in their own personal spiritual formation. Thus the course focuses significantly on some of the inner aspects of leadership, and only secondly on some specific outward leadership skills and disciplines. We want to set before people a vision for service and leadership and thus to train a larger pool of leaders than we actually need (thereby, hopefully, averting the regular crises of having to recruit for under-resourced ministries). We also want to establish a clear set of values at the heart of those who will be the prime influencers over the rest of the church.

The course consists of nine monthly evening sessions, each of which contains some input from the front, some time to process stuff together in small groups and apply it to our own context, and some time to pray for one another (we want all our leaders to be confident in ministering to others in the power of the Spirit). Every participant is provided with a mentor (who has previously completed the course) for the duration of the course and meets with them each month to process further lessons learned. Not only does the content of the individual sessions provide valuable teaching, but the opportunity for you, as senior leader, to input regularly into the lives of your key and emerging leaders is also very significant for you and for them.

There are a wide variety of other opportunities these days for leaders to access other training resources, whether online, through attending conferences, or in all manner of other ways. I make a point of allocating a generous amount of money from our church budget each year for training of those involved in ministry and leadership. This enables us to subsidize attendance at conferences for those who give a good deal of time and energy to resourcing ministry in our church, and also to bring in practitioners from outside to teach and train us in areas in which we aspire to grow.

## GROWING A LEADERSHIP CULTURE

*I think leaders are at their very best when they are raising up leaders around them or, put another way, leaders are at their best when they are creating a leadership culture. I am convinced that leaders must make this one of their highest leadership priorities, because only leaders can develop other leaders and create a leadership culture.*[27]

A leadership culture is one in which everyone understands that they have the potential to exercise kingdom influence, whether through some formal ministry area in the life of the church, or in their workplace or in some other context. It is a culture in which everyone understands that the Spirit has been poured out on every believer[28] and that He intends to manifest Himself through every believer for the good of others.[29] Churches which manage to grow such a culture are churches that exert exceptional influence in their communities because they have succeeded in mobilizing a high proportion of their membership for ministry.

Not only will they be imaginative in responding to the various opportunities for mission presented by their unique context, but their members will always be on the lookout for opportunities to partner with God in His kingdom work in the cut and thrust of everyday life. They will be those who find themselves praying with unchurched friends over coffee as those friends open up about their lives. They will be the ones who set the tone and who shape the atmosphere in school governing body meetings. They will be the ones to whom others look for a lead in community groups because they are known for their wise and servant-hearted leadership. Moreover, these will be churches which begin to shape the wider church because their commitment to raising up and developing leaders is not confined simply to resourcing their own local ministry. They see themselves as seedbeds for ministry and leadership, and love to nurture and grow leaders who might lead or even plant churches elsewhere. Stephen Cottrell observes:

> *The secret of effective leadership here seems to involve having an eye on a larger goal: the affirmation, training and mobilisation of others. In which case one of the main tasks of leadership is to identify and nurture those who will not only take the organisation forward but in due course take it over.*[30]

This is costly. Although most of me rejoiced when we saw some of our best new believers grow in leadership to such an extent that they went off to lead churches themselves, part of me thought it might have been good to have been spared the hard work of having to raise up yet more people to fill the gaps they left!

To see such a culture develop and grow requires a steely determination – especially on the part of the senior leader – to prioritize the development of people rather than merely the doing of tasks. To return to our initial image, it requires the leader to turn their back for a moment on the fire in order to wake up the firemen. This is a hard thing to do for a number of reasons. Our instinct is to respond to the urgent, especially if the urgent is also important. It takes determination to keep reminding ourselves that by giving it less attention in the short term we are massively increasing capacity in the longer term and giving ourselves an even chance of seeing the blaze put out. It means resisting the pressures which come from both within and without to spend our time on things which may make us or others feel good but which ultimately don't move the kingdom agenda forward.

Still, in some churches, there will be an expectation that the minister will spend much of their time engaged in pastoral ministry (that is, pandering to the whims of some established church members). While I have always been prepared to respond to genuine and critical pastoral situations, I have been clear that my priority has to be the raising up of others in order to extend the scope of the ministry we are able to offer (including pastoral ministry). The eminently quotable John Wimber used to comment, "It is not the overall leader's job to do everything, but it is the leader's job to make sure that everything is done!"

I am convinced that the only way I can ensure that everything is done and that we increase our capacity as a church to accomplish yet more, is for me to stop doing tasks and to prioritize developing and overseeing other leaders (who are, anyway, probably better than I could ever be in the areas of responsibility in which they are gifted!). It may be that we lose capacity in the short term, as the leader turns away deliberately from less productive but more visible tasks in order to focus on investing in others. However, before long, such investment will pay off massively and will lead to far greater capacity and vastly increased fruitfulness.

As John Maxwell puts it:

> *Not having enough time to teach another person to do a job is probably the most common reason people give for not delegating. And not delegating is probably the most common reason people don't have enough time. Inability to delegate due to lack of time is short-term thinking. Time lost in delegating on the front end is recovered at the back end.*[31]

Our priorities as senior leaders will now include not only talent spotting of emerging leaders and the equipping and training of all leaders. We must also be able to hand over areas of ministry with appropriate accountability (along with a willingness for things to be done less well in the short term!), going out of our way to encourage those who are taking on leadership, and allocating significant time to supervising and managing other leaders (more of this in the next chapter).

This will be a challenge to some of us and to our inherited models of ministry and leadership. Not only have some been raised and trained in a culture which suggests that all ministry and leadership is essentially the province of the priest or pastor, but, to be brutally honest, some of us find our affirmation and sense of worth through working to meet the needs and expectations of others. The trouble is, this is not the way in which Jesus ministered Himself nor is it the pattern He left for those who followed after Him. If we are to be faithful to His blueprint for ministry and leadership then, in the immortal words of Bill Hybels, we will commit ourselves to becoming DOPs (developers of people) rather than DOTs (doers of tasks)!

**FURTHER READING AND RESOURCES**

Mike Breen, *Multiplying Missional Leaders*, Pawley's Island, SC: 3DM, 2012

James Lawrence, *Growing Leaders*, Oxford: BRF, 2004

John C. Maxwell, *Developing the Leaders Around You*, Nashville, TN: Nelson, 1995

Jo Owen, *How to Lead*, Harlow: Pearson Education, 2009

## Growing Leaders

We have already mentioned the CPAS Growing Leaders courses and other related resources. Their website contains details of these plus some of the best materials available to do with mentoring others: http://www.cpas.org.uk/church-resources/growing-leaders-suite/growing-leaders

## S.H.A.P.E. Course

One of the most helpful tools we have consistently used over the years, as a way of helping people find appropriate ways of engaging in ministry in church and community, has been the S.H.A.P.E. course developed by Saddleback Church in California. Participants are taken on a journey of appraisal in terms of the five key components which "shape" them for particular ministry (Spiritual gifts, Heart/passion, Abilities/skills, Personality, Experiences). After building up a more comprehensive picture of their own shape they are then invited to meet for a Shape interview with a church leader and to discuss possible areas of service in which they would be a good fit. This course can be run over a series of weeks, or as a day conference. Details of the original version can be found at http://www.saddlebackresources.com/collections/shape though a number of more "anglicized" redactions are circulating informally across some networks of churches.

# 7
# Organizing For Growth:
# Developing Functional Structures

If the decline of the Church is ultimately caused neither by the irrelevance of Jesus, nor by the indifference of the community, but by the church's failure to respond fast enough to an evolving culture, to a challenging spiritual climate, and to the promptings of the Holy Spirit, then that decline can be addressed by the repentance of the Church. For true repentance involves turning round and living in a new way in the future... which may lead to growth in numbers and strength because the Spirit of Jesus has been released to do his work.[1]

I am critical of institutionalism... only because through my study of the phenomenal Jesus movements I have come to the unnerving conclusion that God's people are more potent by far when they have little of what we would recognize as church institution in their life together.[2]

I am a relatively recent convert to gardening. I took it up a few years ago mainly because it was Nadine, my wife's, principal hobby and favoured mode of relaxation, and it seemed a good idea to try to develop a hobby we could share together (she having shown no enthusiasm for taking up cricket!). I rapidly became hooked, though equally rapidly realized that, unlike Nadine, who loves growing flowers and shrubs, for me, the only things worth growing were those you could eat! So, I dug vegetable beds, erected a polytunnel, and planted an orchard. Gardening is good for the humility, I discovered. It doesn't take a gardener long to realize that we have no innate capacity whatsoever to make anything grow. The best we can do is to provide the right conditions to enable the life that is latent within seeds to burst forth and to enable plants to thrive. There is plenty we can do to thwart both those processes, and if we don't clear the ground of weeds and pests, if we don't provide water and nutrients, if we don't prune bushes and trees at the right time, then we will very likely actually prevent our garden from becoming productive.

Gardening has given me lots of insights into church leadership. The two have a great deal in common. Contrary to what some books might suggest, none of us can actually make our churches, or any of their members, grow. This seems to be exactly what the apostle Paul is at pains to point out to the Corinthians when he insists that though he and others have tended the church rather like gardeners, it is only God who can give the growth.[3] However, just like a seed or a plant, the church is a living organism which does carry within itself the expectation that it will grow.[4] Indeed, a church which is not growing should be seen as somehow unusual and should lead us to ask questions as to what might be hindering its natural activity. Church leaders are thus called to act as careful gardeners, working in partnership with God to foster and steward the growth which He initiates. Our job is to make sure that we are creating the right environment in which that growth might take place and clearing the ground of anything that might hinder such growth.

Back in the 1990s, Christian Schwarz, a researcher into church growth and development, conducted perhaps the most comprehensive study ever undertaken into the causes of church growth.[5] He surveyed thousands of churches in thirty-two different countries, across every continent, some large and some much smaller, and in every conceivable context. His research questionnaire left him the task of processing more than 4 million answers to questions asked.

His conclusions have proved to be immensely helpful for subsequent generations of churches and their leaders, giving simple yet profound insights into the factors which affect church growth and decline. Working from the conviction that God is the sole author of church growth, and likening the task of church leadership to that of a gardener, Schwarz's research convinced him that there were eight "quality characteristics" common to all growing churches in every context. If churches worked hard to see these qualities expressed in their own context, then they would produce an environment in which God's church was free to grow and thrive. However, if any one of these eight characteristics is neglected or absent, then that church's capacity to thrive and grow is seriously compromised. Schwarz summarizes his conclusions by suggesting that:

> *We should not attempt to manufacture church growth, but rather to release the biotic potential which God has put into every church. It is our task to minimise the obstacles to growth and multiplication within churches. Then church growth can happen "all by itself" as God has promised.*[6]

The quality characteristics which Schwarz identifies should not surprise us. Some describe the quality of the life of the local church: "passionate spirituality", "inspiring worship", "loving relationships". Others refer to the ministry and leadership in which the church engages: "empowering leadership", "gift-orientated ministry", "need-orientated evangelism". However, two of the eight deal directly with the structures of the church – the way the local church organizes itself. If we are serious about the business of turning churches round and enabling them to grow numerically and in quality of life, then we will need, before too long, to assess the way the church is structured and ask hard questions about how far those structures serve, or actually hinder, the core purpose for which the church exists.

Specifically, we need to make sure, insists Schwarz, that the church which we lead has *functional* structures. Let me reiterate what I suggested in an earlier chapter. Changing structures by itself without changing the hearts of people will not accomplish the turnaround of a local church. However, failure to change structures which are not helpful or functional will ultimately hinder the business of helping people to grow and become fruitful, and will hold back the forward movement of the church.

In talking about structures, we are referring to the way the church organizes itself for such activities as worship, disciple-making, governance, leadership, and ministry. It may well be that the church we have begun to lead or in which we find ourselves is one whose structures actually take little cognizance of the need for some of these functions (usually disciple-making and any ministry to those outside the existing church family). Our greatest frustrations may be around the ways in which the existing structures fail to further the purpose for which the church is called to exist.

Winston Churchill once memorably quipped, "We shape our buildings; thereafter they shape us." The same could equally be said of organizational structures. The historic denominations all emerged in a context in which the primary aspiration of the church was to teach the faithful and to prevent them from falling into error (or into the hands of other Christian groups!). The church structures which emerged in those days, and which have remained subsequently largely unchanged, may well have been suitable for the accomplishment of the purposes for which they were developed and may well have been appropriate in an age in which it was assumed that virtually everyone subscribed to the Christian faith. However, in a missional context in which the vast majority of the population have no understanding of, let alone commitment to, the Christian good news, those structures are no longer appropriate. They are also often a stranglehold on the life of the church, preventing it from fulfilling the task to which God is calling it and slowly killing it. As C. S. Lewis observes:

> *There exists in every church something that sooner or later works against the very purpose for which it came into existence. So we must strive very hard, by the grace of God, to keep the church focused on the mission that Christ originally gave to it.[7]*

But because these are the very structures which have exclusively shaped the experience of church for many of those who are still left, and because they represent the last point of connection with a dimly remembered, more flourishing age, people are reluctant to abandon them. Indeed, the structures themselves are what give meaning and significance to some for whom the church is primarily an organization rather than a mission movement. The structures we once shaped now shape us and squeeze us into their mould. Christian Schwarz observes that traditionalism – a weddedness to a past way of doing things – is a polar opposite to the quality characteristic of functional structures:

> *Our research confirmed for the first time an extremely negative relationship between traditionalism and both growth and quality within the church. Almost two thirds of declining churches are plagued by the problem of being tradition-bound.[8]*

I still recall trying to help an Anglican minister who had come to me some years ago for advice about the leadership of the three village churches he had taken on. Each had a congregation of fewer than twenty people, yet each had the structures and apparatus of a much larger church. I suggested to him that rather than seeing himself as the minister of three "cathedrals" (the role into which he was being effectively forced), he would do better to see himself as the overseer of three lifegroups, each charged with responsibility for reaching the wider community for Christ. If each small congregation adopted the more flexible outlook and structure of a small group, then not only would they be far more likely to have an impact in their communities, but their vicar would be spared the breakdown towards which he was surely heading!

We were not meant to exist for nor be shaped by existing structures; rather, we were meant to see structures as provisional and always to reshape them according to our current missional needs. It is always worth asking the question, "Given the calling which we have from God, and given our core purpose as a church, if we were starting out from scratch, would we structure things according to our current pattern?" If the answer to this question is "No", or "Not entirely", then perhaps we ought to re-examine our existing structures in the light of our true calling.

In this chapter, I am not primarily going to be addressing the issue of how we begin to change these structures. In many ways this has been tackled in the earlier chapters. Structures follow vision and the reorientation of a church around the missional purposes of God. Rather, I am going to focus on what these structures might actually look like, and set out some ideas of structures we might aspire to replicate or at least improvise around. This is necessary if we are to lead a church which takes seriously the business of growing missional disciples, growing capacity for ministry and leadership, and helping people encounter God in worship.

Let me also say, at the outset, that all structures, including those which we establish ourselves, have to be seen as provisional, as meeting the needs of the current situation in which we find ourselves, but always open to the possibility of being revised or replaced as our situation and its requirements change. In a turnaround situation they may well be evolutionary, moving steadily but gradually from inherited form to a more functional form. It may take us a number of years to arrive at structures with which we are truly satisfied.

## GROWING MISSIONAL DISCIPLES

We have already commented on the disproportionate amount of time and energy Jesus expended in growing disciples in order to multiply His own mission and ministry, and the way He structured His own ministry to that end. If we are to give similar priority to making and releasing disciples then we will, first of all, need to develop appropriate structures to enable this to happen. Above all, this will mean establishing a network of small groups in which people are enabled to grow in missional discipleship.

Christian Schwarz's research suggests that all eight quality characteristics are vital for the effective functioning of the local church. However, he insists that:

> *If we were to identify any one principle as the most important then without a doubt it would be the multiplication of small groups... These must be holistic groups which go beyond simply discussing Bible passages, to applying its spiritual message in daily life. In these groups, members are able to bring*

*up the issues and questions that are their immediate*
*personal concerns... and these groups are the*
*natural place for Christians to learn to serve others*
*– both inside and outside the group – with their*
*spiritual gifts.*[9]

Small groups, whether lifegroups, cell groups or whatever you wish to call them, have to become the building blocks of the church, the primary unit for growth in every aspect of discipleship. They will be places where each member of the group plays a part in encouraging one another in growth in relationship with God, in living life faithfully and well, in taking hold of all of the resources which God gives us as we navigate our way through life's challenges, and in our witness to those who are not yet integrated into God's kingdom. They will be places where people are held accountable for their own personal growth, where people are prayed for, supported, and encouraged as they journey with God. They will be places where people gain confidence in serving and in personal witness and take encouragement from having others, preferably in similar life situations, to journey with. Although I am sure that people miss out if they are not regularly part of larger gatherings for worship and teaching, and think that people grow best if they are committed to both aspects of local church life, if I am brutally honest, and if people were only able to commit to one church gathering each week, then I would rather people were actively involved in a small group than in the larger Sunday gathering. In both the churches I have led I have spent a good deal of my energies in the early years establishing a functional network of small groups.

In Saltburn this was clearly going to take a little time, as there was no culture of small groups in the history of the church. For them to be effective, and for them to achieve the purposes for which they were intended, it was vital that the right DNA be embedded deep within them from the outset. Responsibility for this can only lie with the overall leader of the church. Our weekly Open to God meeting was our vehicle for gathering those who were spiritually hungry and helping them move forward along the path of discipleship. I wanted to bring these people together in a context where I could shape them around God's word, help them grow in a sense of God's call, and encourage them to join in with God's mission in full reliance on the power of His Spirit. I remain utterly convinced that the first and most important thing to do in a turnaround situation is to create a space in which people are given opportunity to grow in this way and to begin to experience something more of God's presence and power. This is our best opportunity as overall leader to shape the spiritual life of the church and of its people, to extend ownership of the vision for the church which God has entrusted to us, and to begin to identify, raise up, and develop emerging leaders.

After three years, this meeting had grown numerically, and the people attending had grown in all manner of ways. The DNA was understood and owned widely, and a small group of leaders had emerged. We continued to meet fortnightly all together but now, on alternate weeks, we met in four small groups, each one led by a lay member of the church in partnership with an associate (or trainee) leader whom they were developing. Within three years the number of small groups had doubled as groups grew and multiplied.

Arriving in All Saints, our current church, we were faced with a slightly different situation. Although we inherited a number of "housegroups", there was little sense of connectedness between them and the rest of the life of the church. Each tended to do its own thing. Meetings by and large centred around Bible studies which were fairly cerebral, the make up of groups had not really changed (in some cases for years), and if the members were not tired and a little disillusioned, then most of the leaders certainly were! When, at an early meeting of leaders, I tentatively suggested that the whole system might be in need of an overhaul, roughly half of the leaders, sensing an easy way out, enthusiastically offered their resignation!

For much of my first year in post, I taught about the values of missional discipleship and about how these might best be advanced through an effective system of holistic small groups. As well as preaching on Sundays, I hosted a number of midweek meetings in which we explained how such groups might operate, what it would mean to be part of such a group, and cast a vision for a church *of* small groups as opposed to one *with* small groups. These groups were going to be the primary carriers of the DNA of the church, so it was vital to find leaders for them who really had that DNA and who got the vision for what we were seeking to accomplish.

As had been the case several years earlier in Saltburn, I looked for people whom I felt might have the capacity and the heart to shape others and to help others grow. Many of them had not really seen themselves as potential small group leaders (assuming that such leaders had to have particular intellectual or theological skills in which they personally felt lacking). I then formed a prototype lifegroup of all of these leaders which met for three months[10] under my leadership. I modelled the kind of small group leadership I wanted to see proliferate throughout the church, introduced each member of the group to leadership, coached them along the way, and reflected with them on the different elements of small group life. We then engaged in a complex process of forming a number of lifegroups, inviting people to indicate two or three people whom they would most like to be with in a group, and trying to form groups which were sufficiently homogenous to have a good chance of thriving and growing.

Without any shadow of a doubt, this has been one of the most significant factors in the subsequent growth of All Saints and in the growth of a culture in which everyone has an understanding of being called by God to engage in His mission. It has been the context in which people have grown in ministry skills and confidence, out of which entirely new ministries have been birthed, and in which leaders have been identified and developed.

The whole system had another complete overhaul after eight or nine years. For some time we had been increasingly shaped by the wonderful insights into "whole life discipleship" which had been developed by the London Institute of Contemporary Christianity.[11] We wanted people to have opportunity to be part of lifegroups along with others who had similar missional concerns. We asked all our church members to answer a simple question: what do you see as your own frontline, the place where you are especially called by God to exercise influence for His kingdom? For some this was their workplace, for others the school gate, and for others a local walking group. We encouraged people to form groups with others who shared a similar frontline, who understood similar pressures, challenges, and missional opportunities.

This was a much more evolutionary approach to small group formation but has been remarkably effective. We have been able to be far more successful in resourcing those with heavy work commitments (one group, formed of people who work away from home during the week, meets via Skype!). We have also seen an explosion in terms of mission to mothers and young families, as a number of parents who regularly met at the school gate formed a small group together, ran a series of Alpha courses for other young mums, began other associated missional initiatives, and now have spawned a network of related lifegroups.

Each cluster of loosely related small groups is overseen by a missional community leader who meets regularly (every four to six weeks) with his or her cluster of small group leaders. These meetings will be partly to offer practical support and to address any issues to do with the groups, but are principally focused on the development of the leaders. These missional community leaders meet similarly on a monthly basis with the senior church leader. It goes without saying that this is a brilliant way of ensuring that the core DNA of the church is reinforced and proliferates throughout the whole church. It is also the only way I know, in a church of whatever size, to ensure that everyone enjoys a proper sense of belonging and is able to make several significant relationships. I once heard an effective small group structure described as being the only sure way of shutting the back door of the church!

What's it like to be part of a lifegroup? Let's go along with Dave to his group.

To be honest, Dave had been half inclined not to go at all this evening. His recent promotion as Head of Year in the school where he has worked for the last five years has meant even more evening meetings; he could really do with the time to finish off his lesson planning for tomorrow; and, frankly, he is feeling pretty exhausted after having to initiate, this afternoon, the exclusion from school of a difficult pupil. However, he feels something of a responsibility towards the others in the group. Most of them are also in pretty high-pressure work contexts and in recent weeks they have really journeyed together, praying for one another as several group members have had to negotiate their way through some tough situations at work. They are the people who most of all relate to some of the pressures Dave has to face, and being with them always leaves him feeling refreshed, energized, and understood.

Sonia, who leads the group, has called everyone to order, and the general catching up with each other quietens down as she asks if there are any immediate needs for prayer — that is, things people just have to get off their chest before they can properly concentrate on the evening ahead. Dave mentions his concern about the excluded pupil (not a welcome situation, probably unavoidable, but one which he has agonized over ever since leaving school earlier). A few gather round Dave and pray for him; someone has a specific Scripture which Dave finds especially reassuring, and suddenly he is seeing things a bit more clearly and from God's perspective. He loves the simple worship which then follows as one of the group reads a psalm, gives people time to let the words sink in, and then plays a worship song through a music system. The sense of God's presence is very real.

Janet, a lab assistant in another local school, is leading the Bible-based part of the evening. For the last four weeks, the group members have all read the letter to the Ephesians at least once each week, and each week have shared not only what God has spoken to them, but more importantly what they feel He is asking them to do by way of response. Tonight the group is using some questions prepared by last Sunday's preacher, who introduced a new series on the life of David. The questions are simple:

- How did God speak to you through last Sunday's teaching and how has this affected you subsequently?

- What most encouraged you from the teaching and what most challenged you? Why?

- What do you think God is asking you to do as a result of what you heard?

- In what specific ways, as a result of this evening's study, would you most like God to help you?

- In groups of three, pray for one another, inviting God's Spirit to come and minister to each of us the help we need.

A few weeks ago the group compiled a list of names of people to pray for, each member contributing the names of two or three friends who are not yet in the kingdom and whom they long to see come to Christ. Dave has prayed for his brother Steve, and for his best mate, Andy, for years, though with no apparent effect! It's so great to have others praying for them too, now; it shares the load! Sometimes the group will pray through the list together towards the end of the meeting, and ask one another questions about what contact they are having with those for whom they are praying and whom they are seeking to reach. However, this evening they are choosing to do one of their other regular exercises designed to encourage one another in the outward dimension of discipleship.

Sonia has put a chair in the middle of the room and asked Pete, an accountant, to sit on it. Pete is now asked to describe his own frontline situation and the challenges and opportunities he faces. He talks about his office, his work colleagues, about the difficulty in getting time just to hang out together given the pressure of the workday, and about a forthcoming three-day work appointment in London. The rest of the group ask him a few searching questions, offer some counsel in some of the areas he has raised, and then gather round, at Sonia's invitation, to lay hands on Pete, and to pray prophetically over him. Dave really appreciated being on the receiving end of similar prayer himself a few weeks ago, and knows that Pete will go into work tomorrow feeling a fresh sense of God's calling on his life and a renewed sense of being commissioned as God's ambassador to his own workplace.

It's late when Dave gets home, and he still has planning to do for tomorrow. But as he settles down to get it done, it doesn't feel quite so much like a chore, rather a partnership with God in the great work of seeing His kingdom grow in the school to which God has called Dave to be His representative.

## A CLEAR WAY IN

As the church begins to engage more readily with its community, and as people begin to be intrigued by the new life they see expressed in its members, hopefully there will begin to be a trickle of people who want to explore questions of faith. Sunday worship, especially if it is still of a rather traditional bent, may well not be the most helpful context for such exploration to take place. It's vital that a church has a spiritual maternity ward in which faith and spiritual life can be birthed and in which people can find answers to their questions, encounter God, and begin to take their first steps with Him. Some lifegroups may run Alpha or other similar introductory courses for their own friends and contacts. However, it is always good to run at least one such course centrally each year and to feed people into it as they express interest. We have sometimes found it helpful to ask a specific lifegroup to help in the practical running of an Alpha course, with a view to them building relationship over the weeks with the newcomers attending, and then to incorporate those newcomers into their lifegroup at the end of the course.

The pressure exerted by the raft of responsibilities and expectations which a church may wish to impose upon its minister can very easily mean that new initiatives (such as running an Alpha course) can be pushed to one side, especially if only a small number of people are showing any interest in attending. However, if we have any aspiration whatsoever to welcome new and previously unchurched people into our church, then this really is an activity we are going to have to prioritize. Furthermore, because our structures do express something of what we believe to be important about the church, establishing some form of structured ministry for enquirers flags up the fact that this is a church which takes seriously the business of helping seekers find faith.

## BUILDING LEADERSHIP CAPACITY

One of the leadership observations that has had the most profound effect on me over the years is one I read shortly before my own ordination, which was made by a South American Roman Catholic priest. He ventured the opinion that every minister going into a new post should go with the aim of doing themselves out of a job within three years. That, he suggested, is exactly what Jesus did! Although churches may well always need a senior leader who will take responsibility for the development of ministry and who might be a catalyst for new initiatives, the more responsibilities we hold on to ourselves, the less scope there will be for growth to take place. The first priority for a leader, therefore, is not simply to do ministry tasks, but rather to engage in the building of leadership capacity by raising up and investing in other leaders.

Alongside this we need to develop structures which promote such ongoing multiplication of leadership. This will inevitably mean building a leadership team with whom leadership might be shared. Out of the various different models we might adopt for forming a leadership team, there is only one which I have found to be truly effective, especially in the early stages of growing a church: to form a team composed of the different heads of ministry areas in the church. How might we go about this?

## Identifying ministry leaders

I often suggest to church leaders that they engage in the following exercise.

On a piece of blank paper write down three columns. In the first column list the different core ministry areas reflected in the life of your church or which you hope to see expressed in the near future. This might include such ministries as teaching, disciple-making, evangelism, youth, children, prayer ministry, worship, pastoral ministry, ministry to the elderly, and administration. In the second column, write down the name of the person who is currently directly responsible for the oversight and direction of this ministry (the person who recruits and oversees other leaders, and who acts as champion for the development of the ministry). You may well find that your own name features a number of times in this column. Now, in the third column, write down the name of the person whom you think ought to be the champion and overseer of this ministry. This may be someone who is only just beginning to demonstrate a passion for the ministry or who has only recently begun to get involved with it but whom God is clearly gifting to develop it. These are the people in whom you might want to invest particular time and energy in growing, developing, and resourcing for leadership of their ministry areas. I have often given extra time over a limited period of a few months to working alongside such people in a particular ministry area.

When I first started at All Saints Marple, one of the areas of ministry I identified as being in particular need of reengineering and developing was that of prayer ministry. It's not a particular ministry to which I feel especially called, but I do have some clear views as to the way in which it might most helpfully be undertaken and the values which need to lie at the heart of this ministry. So, for the first year or two, I effectively took responsibility for overseeing prayer ministry. I worked alongside those who were in the ministry team, modelling a somewhat new way of engaging in prayer ministry, and eventually releasing its oversight to someone else who had picked up the vision and values. I will now no longer launch a new ministry initiative with me as overall leader, unless I have alongside me someone else who will take over responsibility for its oversight within a relatively short period of time after having been coached in the core vision and values of that particular ministry.

As you fill in names in this third column, don't worry, by the way, if you need to leave a few blanks. Far better to wait until you have recognized someone who is truly gifted and anointed to take the ministry forward than to fill in someone's name simply for the sake of tidiness! The names in the third column are the foundations of your ministry/ leadership/staff team. If people with a particular passion and giftedness for specific ministries are overseeing those ministries, then there is every chance that those ministries will thrive far more effectively than if you, as senior leader, were left to manage and direct them.

Of course you may end up with a set of names in the third column which are different from those in the second – that is, you have some obvious people who might be well placed to develop particular ministry areas but someone else is currently in some form of positional leadership over those very areas. The challenge facing you is how to help those people move on in order that they might be replaced by someone more suitable. In talking to church leaders concerned about moving a local church forward, the business of leadership transition, and especially of helping some inherited leaders to move on, is one of the most pressing issues they face. There are a number of strategies you might usefully employ. Here are a few I have found to be helpful.

- Introduce a fixed-term tenure for office holders/ ministry leaders. Often people work on the assumption that, when given responsibility within the church, they have been given a job for life. By introducing the practice of reviewing areas of responsibility every three years you can effectively undermine such an assumption and create an understanding that holding office is a more medium-term proposition (even if some people end up holding responsibility for more than one three-year span).

- Establish a system of performance management/ supervision. Agree some basic expectations to do with the undertaking of ministry responsibilities. If a person is not able to deliver on these, then that might indicate that they are not the most suitable person to continue with the responsibility. This gives you a way of helping them move on. I have found that by raising the level of expectation in terms of what responsibility looks like and especially by increasing the expectation of spiritual commitment for office holders, some leaders who really should no longer be in leadership positions have very naturally and amicably withdrawn from leadership.

- Give time to exploring with leaders where their particular passions and skills lie. It may be that someone has taken on a responsibility in the past for noble motives, there having been no one else to fill a gap. It may be that a concerned discussion about what really excites them might result in them being given an opportunity to lay down a responsibility in order to engage in something different but which is far more in keeping with their skill set.

- Be patient. It may take three or four years before you are able to move on everyone from positions where they are more hindrance than help. By allowing things to go at a reasonable pace you may be able to effect smoother and more amicable transitions with less collateral damage than if you set yourself to changing personnel overnight.

Of course, we are not suggesting that people simply be appointed and then left to their own devices in terms of the running of these ministry areas. Your task is to oversee these leaders, resource them, and help them grow in their own leadership, and to help them see how their ministry area relates to the ministry of the whole church. The other good reason for forming a leadership/ministry team in this way is that it has an element of transparency about it. It is absolutely clear why these people are part of this team; this is not merely the minister's "in-group" but rather the gathering of those who have responsibility for all the key ministries in the church.

Although in our current church we have always managed, because of our size, to employ some paid staff in addition to clergy, most of those who have been on our staff team and who have overseen key ministry areas have been unpaid. Throughout the nine years I was in my last church I was the only paid staff member. Some of those who have been on these leadership teams have been in full-time paid employment elsewhere; others have chosen to reduce their paid employment in order to give one or two days to leading (unpaid) in the local church. Some have been early retired, while others have taken the decision, along with their spouse, to live off one income in order to be free to give themselves to leadership in the church. The setting up of a ministry team is not dependent upon having vast financial resources, but rather on having people who are willing to serve.

## Building and resourcing the team

These are the people who are your top priority as senior leader. You need to make sure that you have sufficient time to invest in them, to pastor them, and to help them thrive. Given that they oversee the activities which lie at the heart of the church and its life, these are the ones who have the greatest capacity to shape the ethos and direction of the church. Experience has convinced me that what we cultivate at the core of the church – and this team represents that core – will proliferate throughout the whole church and will infuse every aspect of the church's being. I would recommend meeting with them at least every half-term one to one for a supervision meeting. This meeting (which normally lasts between 60 and 90 minutes) is an opportunity for them to feed back on achievements and challenges, to discuss resourcing needs, and to discuss future vision and planning for the ministry. It is an opportunity for you to help steer the course of the ministry and to help your leaders develop and grow by feeding back on their own performance, by helping them to set some personal development goals and offering resources to them.

It is obviously important that the team has opportunity to meet together, and thus become far more than simply a loose affiliation of individual practitioners. Over the years we have developed a practice of meeting weekly for prayer, business, and diary planning (on Tuesday morning, for those who are not working elsewhere and who are able to meet) and monthly in the evening, in order to enable those who are in other paid employment to attend. Those leading clusters of small groups are also invited to this meeting (as were all small group leaders in our time in Saltburn). The evening meeting includes worship, feedback from one or two ministry leaders on their ministry area, some essential business, but always something of an inspirational, vision-casting or training nature from me as senior leader. This, I always feel, is my principal opportunity to shape those who will shape the life of the church. It is also the place where vision is shaped and refined, where there is opportunity to test out new ideas, and where we can encourage and pray for one another as leaders. It is the place where people are helped to see how their ministry area fits into the whole life and ministry of the church and where people are mutually encouraged.

We have found it invaluable over the years to draw on various resources to build the life of the team and to promote mutual understanding for the different personalities reflected in its members. We have profited from days away together, sometimes for discerning vision together, sometimes for team building. We have found it helpful to explore our various personality profiles using such tools as Myers-Briggs Personality Indicator and the Enneagram.[12] These have been especially useful not only in promoting greater understanding of one another, but also for helping team members understand how different personality types can relate most helpfully to, and bring the best out of, those who might be very different from themselves! We have found it extremely useful to explore the different roles we fulfil on our team by using the Belbin team roles indicator.[13]

We have identified the particular strengths and weaknesses we each bring to the team and have grown to recognize that, not only do some excel in areas where others are weak, but that it is most productive to defer to one another in our respective areas of strength. And one of the highlights of our year is going away as a team to the annual New Wine Leadership conference, where we not only get inspired and energized by great worship, teaching, and ministry (very important for those who spend most of their time giving out), but we also get to hang out and have fun together!

## WORSHIP THAT HELPS PEOPLE ENCOUNTER GOD

Changing the structure or content of Sunday worship services may well present the greatest challenge to the leader who is concerned to turn a church around. For many people, church is all about what happens on Sunday. Indeed, Sunday worship may well represent the sum total of what constitutes spiritual life for many people. Rather than being, as it should be, a corporate expression of a personal walk with God which is nourished by daily encounter with Him through prayer and Bible reading, Sunday worship for many is effectively a substitute for a sustained personal walk. This is one reason why often people are so fiercely invested in maintaining established patterns of Sunday worship.

One of Christian Schwarz's quality characteristics for healthy churches is "inspiring worship services":

> *Whenever the Holy Spirit is truly at work (and his presence is not merely presumed), he will have a concrete effect upon the way a worship service is conducted including the entire atmosphere of a gathering... When worship is inspiring, it draws people to the services "all by itself".[14]*

I suspected that the very traditional worship of Emmanuel Saltburn was not an inspiring experience for many of those who came along week by week, let alone those who were outside the church. We began to discuss possible changes to the pattern of services after a few months, and when more than a few people had begun to experience something of what worship could be through our midweek informal meetings. The principle around which we reshaped our Sunday worship was that of wanting to be more accessible to unchurched people (at the very least this meant a departure from the fairly monochrome diet of communion services).

I confess that Sunday worship continued to be a frustrating experience for me in the early years in Saltburn, as I felt pulled in every direction by different groups of people, some of whom wanted to move forward much faster than we were doing in terms of changing the worship culture, and others who resented any departure from inherited mode. With hindsight, I probably should have initiated much sooner the move which we took after six years to multiply our Sunday morning services. The church was not enormous numerically, and there was plenty of room within the cavernous building for growth. However, we took the decision to move to two very different weekly worship services – a more traditional communion service with a robed choir (though with the same teaching, prayer ministry team, and with a range of music styles), followed by a contemporary service of worship, teaching, and ministry.

In the first few months, both services grew as people gained confidence to invite friends and as a wider range of people found a place in which they could worship in a manner they found inspiring and helpful. Many leaders agonize about changing forms of worship which they find unhelpful yet in which many of their inherited congregation have a strongly vested interest. The progress of change is thus inevitably often painstakingly slow and creates various problems along the way. Far better to start something new alongside the old.

Our structures, which have often evolved and become formalized over centuries, do indeed shape us, and outdated and unhelpful structures can restrict the free flow of life into and out of our churches to others. However, helpful structures which are appropriate to our understanding of our contemporary mission, and which are shaped around kingdom imperatives, can equally serve to fix such priorities at the heart of the life of the local church. This is why getting the right structures is important. This is why we need always to be reappraising and adjusting our structures in the light of our current missional task.

**FURTHER READING AND RESOURCES**

Mark Greene, *Fruitfulness on the Frontline*, Leicester: IVP, 2014

Phil Potter, *The Challenge of Cell Church*, Oxford: BRF, 2001

Laurence Singlehurst, *Loving the Lost*, Eastbourne: Kingsway, 2001

Howard Snyder, *Radical Renewal: The Problem of Wineskins Today*, Eugene, OR: Wipf & Stock, 1996

## Courses for enquirers

There are a range of off-the-peg courses now available for churches to use as a way of helping seekers find faith and begin to grow in discipleship. Easily the most widely used (and most recognizable to those who are not yet part of the church) is the Alpha course, details of which can be found at www.alpha.org

Others include Emmaus, Christianity Explored, and the Pilgrim course. Prerecorded talks can be shown on a screen either in a home or in a larger setting and discussion materials are available to follow up the content of the talk in small groups.

## Managing tips

For those who want to grow in expertise in managing and supervising paid and volunteer staff or others with areas of responsibility in the life of the church, Phil George's excellent website www.managingtips.com is a treasure trove of wisdom and of free downloadable resources. Phil has vast experience in senior management both in the corporate world and also in the voluntary sector and offers an immensely useful (and easy to use!) model for recruiting and supervising workers.

# Sample Worship Questionnaire

Prior to launching a new service in both Emmanuel Saltburn and also All Saints Marple we surveyed the whole congregation in order to canvas opinion on this and on other related matters. This is the questionnaire we used in Marple in 2008. It serves as a good example of how a questionnaire might be helpfully constructed and used both to raise issues with the wider church but also as a tool in discerning the mind of Christ as we seek to move forward.

1. Which services do you currently attend and how frequently?

|  | Weekly | Fortnightly | Monthly | Occasionally | Never |
|---|---|---|---|---|---|
| 8.00 a.m. | ❑ | ❑ | ❑ | ❑ | ❑ |
| 10.30 a.m. | ❑ | ❑ | ❑ | ❑ | ❑ |
| 6.30 p.m. | ❑ | ❑ | ❑ | ❑ | ❑ |
| Evergreens | ❑ | ❑ | ❑ | ❑ | ❑ |

2. How regularly would you like to see these services take place?

|  | Weekly | Fortnightly | Monthly | Occasionally | Never |
|---|---|---|---|---|---|
| 10.30 a.m. All-Age Worship | ❑ | ❑ | ❑ | ❑ | ❑ |
| Morning Worship | ❑ | ❑ | ❑ | ❑ | ❑ |
| Holy Communion | ❑ | ❑ | ❑ | ❑ | ❑ |
| 6.30 p.m. Holy Communion | ❑ | ❑ | ❑ | ❑ | ❑ |
| Celebration | ❑ | ❑ | ❑ | ❑ | ❑ |

3. We are seriously considering establishing an additional Sunday service, most probably of an "All-Age" worship style, in order to increase our capacity. Would it be best to hold this extra service on Sunday morning or afternoon (e.g. at 4 or 4.30 p.m.)?

| Morning | Afternoon | No Preference |
|---------|-----------|---------------|
| ❑ | ❑ | ❑ |

4. If we were to have two morning services (in addition to the existing 8.00 a.m. service) at what time do you think they should take place?

| First Service | | | Second Service | | |
|---|---|---|---|---|---|
| 9.00 | 9.15 | 9.30 | 11.00 | 11.15 | 11.30 |
| ❑ | ❑ | ❑ | ❑ | ❑ | ❑ |

5. If we were to hold a Sunday afternoon service, at what time should it take place? (Leave blank for "No Preference")

_____

_____

6. Which service(s) would you most likely attend?

| First Service | Second Service | Afternoon Service |
|---------------|----------------|-------------------|
| ❑ | ❑ | ❑ |

7. Do you have any other creative ideas or suggestions concerning provision of additional services?

8. What age group are you in

| Under 10 | 10-19 | 20-29 | 30-39 | 40-49 | 50-59 |
|----------|-------|-------|-------|-------|-------|
| ❑ | ❑ | ❑ | ❑ | ❑ | ❑ |

| 60-69 | 70-79 | Over 80 |
|-------|-------|---------|
| ❑ | ❑ | ❑ |

9. How many children under the age of 14 normally accompany you to church?

_____

_____


10. What 4 things do you most value about our current services at All Saints?


11. What 4 things do you least value about our current services?


12. Are there any other needs which you feel are not being met by our services, or any other factors which ought to be considered in planning our services?


13. Are there other aspects which you feel might be helpfully incorporated into our services?

**PREACHING AND TEACHING**

14. How helpful do you usually find the preaching in terms of equipping you in your own Christian walk? (Please circle on the scale below)

Not Helpful    1    2    3    4    5    Extremely Helpful

15. Do you have any comments to make about the scope of our preaching? Are there topics, themes, etc. which you would like to see covered?

16. Are there any other comments you wish to make about worship or preaching?

# 8

## Staying The Course:
## Leadership For The Long Haul

Whenever God moves forward, it is in conflict with many other forces. The Kingdom of God can expand only out of conflict with the Kingdom of darkness. Hate does not surrender easily to love, nor does evil submit quietly to good. When you seize divine moments, there is a spiritual collision, and a part of seizing those moments to the fullest is a willingness to bear the initial impact alone.[1]

Courage is that quality of mind which enables people to encounter danger or difficulty with firmness, or without fear or depression of spirits... The highest degree of courage is seen in the person who is most fearful but refuses to capitulate to it.[2]

I can still remember vividly the first time I ran in a cross-country race. It was in a PE lesson during my first term at high school. The course, through the school grounds, can't have been more than two miles in total, but that was at least one and a half miles longer than any of us eleven-year-olds had ever run before. For most of the class, our experience of running races was confined to the 100-metre sprint at junior school sports days. So it was no surprise when the bulk of the field set off at a blistering pace, adopting the same mentality they always had done when involved in a competitive race – that of running as fast as you could for as long as you could until you crossed the finish line.

Not me though! My favourite character in the comic I read each week was a long-distance runner – "Alf Tupper, the Tough of the Track". And from studying his exploits, I well understood that the secret to success in long-distance running was pacing yourself; that it wasn't so much about how fast you could run but how long you could run for. As I devoured each eagerly awaited instalment of Alf's rise from humble beginnings to winning an Olympic gold medal, I dreamed of following in his footsteps and of having a career just like his. Now, on a cold November morning, here was my chance not just to dream but (in my imagination, at least!) actually to *be* my comic book hero! So, as most of my classmates tore off at breakneck speed, armed with all the wisdom I had gleaned from a year's worth of comic-strip stories, I adopted Alf's distinctive stance and settled into a measured and sustainable pace. How unfair it was, I remember thinking, for my poor classmates, to be pitched against someone who had Alf Tupper as his inspiration and coach!

I overtook the first group of panting, and by now half-walking, classmates after a few hundred yards. Others I passed clutching their sides with a stitch a little further along the course. As the course turned uphill, along the school drive, still others began to fall by the wayside or to drop down to a walking pace. I didn't actually win that race, but I was one of the first to finish, and did far better than some of my friends who never managed to complete the course. Satisfaction indeed, especially for one who had never been much of a sprinter and who was used to coming last in sports day races.

I grew to love cross-country running during my high school career, and, despite never being anything other than a very moderate athlete, thoroughly enjoyed the experience of representing our school competitively.

Distance running, however, gave me something much more useful. Although I couldn't have known it at the time, with hindsight it provided me with insights, and formed in me attitudes and disciplines, which have proved invaluable in my subsequent leadership career. My experience of ministry has taught me that leading a church, especially through the kind of progression we have been exploring in this book, has much in common with cross-country running. It is certainly more a marathon than a sprint, and along the way there will be a whole host of challenges and hazards with massive potential to stall us and to throw us off course, even to knock us out of the race altogether. I have discovered that races are won or lost in our hearts and minds; that mindset and attitude matter far more than merely physical strength or energy. I have discovered, too, that we are most vulnerable to succumbing to such challenges when our resources are depleted and when we have failed to live at a sustainable pace.

## LONG-DISTANCE MINDSET

Effective leaders are always focused on seeing vision come to fruition. There is often about them a healthy restlessness and a refusal to settle for the status quo. When properly harnessed, this tendency means that there will always be forward momentum in the churches they lead. However, the danger of restlessness when left unchecked is that it causes leaders to begin to resemble my high school classmates and to feel that everything needs to be accomplished overnight. They rush headlong into things at a breathless pace. This approach is usually guaranteed not only to exhaust the leader, but also to ensure that all but a few followers will be left behind, assuming, that is, that they join the race in the first place. It is an oft-repeated, but accurate, observation that many people overestimate what they can achieve in one year, but underestimate what they might achieve in five years. Turning churches round is principally an exercise in seeing a culture changed, and culture change does not happen overnight. What is more, our aspiration has to be to see a culture established that will outlast us and our own leadership span and to see mission and ministry birthed which is sustainable not simply in the short term.

Although Nehemiah's strategic leadership oversaw the rebuilding of the walls of Jerusalem in the remarkably swift time of only fifty-two days, there was nothing hurried about his approach. Indeed, as we have noted previously, he did not even broach the subject of rebuilding until he had undertaken a thorough survey of the state of the city, made detailed plans and preparations, including securing necessary resources and materials, and got the majority of people on board with his great scheme. Given that he was building to secure a longer-term future, and not simply throwing up a temporary structure which might have a rather limited lifespan, there had to be a good deal of care taken in the whole of the building process. This was a painstaking and methodical process.

The same is true when it comes to rebuilding or reengineering churches. Solid foundations need to be laid, a process which does not allow the taking of shortcuts. It may well be the case that in the early stages of rebuilding there may not be a huge amount to show for our efforts. I remember the frustration of not seeing a single new person come to faith through the ministry of our church throughout the whole of our first year in Saltburn. It takes a good deal of time and a fair bit of repetition, in my experience, for most people to own values and vision which may be new or strange to them.

Running too far ahead of people may well compromise the

longer-term stability of the enterprise, however. Our goal is not simply to get people to do the right things, but to help people discern what are the right things to do. We will need to run at their pace. The simple truth is this: turnarounds take time, and those of us who are called to such a ministry need to commit ourselves to settling in for a good length of time in order to see the job through.

Possibly the thing that gave me greatest satisfaction in terms of my time as vicar of Emmanuel Church actually took place after I had left Saltburn. For a variety of reasons (principally to do with diocesan policy) Emmanuel Church was without a vicar, or any other paid staff, for almost two years after I had left. During this time, the church was effectively led by the lay leadership team we had seen come into being in our later years there, and during this time the church continued to grow. One of my greatest joys was to meet up with my former church at the following year's New Wine summer conference and to meet people in their group whom I had never previously met but who had come to faith and been added to the church during the previous year. It was a powerful reminder to me that our calling as leaders is to build for a future beyond our own time in office. Indeed, for those of us engaged in reengineering leadership, or any other similar enterprise, some of our greatest efforts may well bear fruit after we have moved on and others may well benefit most from our hard work.

One of my close friends is an Anglican bishop in one of the more remote and impoverished parts of Uganda. It's an area where many struggle to support themselves, where local churches have few resources, and where their pastors are usually not able to be paid at a level sufficient to maintain themselves and their families. My friend Cranmer has an ambition to plant 100,000 pine trees over the next few years as a cash crop (at the time of writing he is roughly halfway to realizing his ambition). The trees can be planted at the cost of a few pence each, but when harvested, the wood they provide for construction work can be sold for quite a considerable sum. At a conservative estimate, the anticipated harvest could not only contribute significantly to the support of existing clergy, but also enable the training and maintenance of many more pastors and evangelists and the launch of many more new ministry initiatives.

What I find most remarkable about my friend's scheme is that he stands not to benefit from it at all. The trees take fifteen years to come to maturity, by which time he will be retired. However, his successors will benefit hugely from the foresight of this man and will have undreamed of resources at their disposal. I find it helpful to have in mind as a church leader that I am building not simply for my own span of leadership but also for the time when any successor takes over. This in itself frees us from the tyranny of feeling that we have to see everything accomplished during our own incumbency! The apostle Paul well understood this principle when he points out to the Corinthians, "I planted, Apollos watered, but God was causing the growth."[3]

Those who are able to embrace such a mindset realize that the quality they need to prize more highly than most is that of perseverance – the ability to keep going, and to keep others going, irrespective of circumstance or situation. Only those who are able to develop the discipline of perseverance will be able to see genuine culture change come about in the churches they are leading.

## STAYING THE COURSE

It is fascinating to see how frequently the New Testament writers encourage and exhort their first-century audience to steadfastness and perseverance. Jesus reminds His first followers that it is those who will endure to the end who will be saved,[4] while the apostle Paul prays frequently that the churches for whom he is responsible would be "strengthened with all power... so that you may have great endurance and patience".[5] In encouraging the Thessalonians he holds up the steadfastness of Christ[6] as an example and inspiration to them, while in writing to Timothy he lists the very same quality as one which is required of all Christian ministers.[7] The epistle to the Hebrews is in many ways an exhortation to Christians under pressure to persevere at all costs, and, once again, the writer brings his argument to a climax by pointing to the example of Jesus, the ultimate leader of kingdom change, who, despite enormous personal cost, and in the face of immense pressure, *endured* the cross and persevered in running the race set before Him.[8]

It doesn't take too much imagination to understand that the reason that perseverance is so fiercely encouraged by these early Christian writers is that they well understood that those who follow Christ, and especially those who are called to lead in His church, are bound to experience difficulties and challenges. Wise leaders see through the illusion into which much contemporary, Western, Christian culture wants to habituate us — that comfort and ease are automatic signs of God's favour and, somehow, the right of every faithful Christian servant. This is a far cry from the insight of Paul that "all those who desire to live godly in Christ Jesus will be persecuted",[9] or the clear promise of Jesus that in the world His followers would have trouble.[10] The principal difference between Nehemiah and those who had gone before him was exactly this capacity to endure hardship and to keep going even in the face of significant threats and troubles. Others had sought to do exactly what he ended up accomplishing but had lacked the courage and determination which sustained him.

The work of the kingdom will inevitably provoke opposition, both human and spiritual. Those who aspire to break ground for God will always come up against threats and challenges. Some of us may already be all too aware of the reality of this in our own ministries! Let's explore what some of the commonest challenges might be to our staying the course, and then finish by reminding ourselves of what might be some of the secrets to perseverance.

## FACING THE CHALLENGES

### Human opposition

There will always be those who readily embrace the new work of the Spirit which we are seeking to bring into the life of our church, and others who will gradually get on board with things. However, there will always be those who are at best unhappy with our leadership or who, at worst, make it their business to oppose it at all costs. This can be for all manner of reasons.

For some people, a new set of vision and values and a whole new understanding of the fundamental purpose of the church threatens their own positional leadership or the power base they have cultivated for themselves over the years. When Nehemiah began his work of rebuilding, the first people to complain and to pour scorn on his work were the local tribal leaders and power-brokers for whom the re-emergence of a rebuilt Jerusalem constituted a threat to their own influence and position.[11] These are the very people[12] who have previously been responsible for the rebuilding work to be halted and who pose a very real threat in the minds of the people of Jerusalem. Nehemiah's challenge is not simply to stay focused in terms of completing the task of rebuilding but also to maintain morale among a fragile people.

Opposition may be challenging to us but it can be devastating to those who are beginning to follow us. Especially in the early stages of leadership for change, we need to keep careful watch over those who are beginning to move forward with us and pay special attention to their support and encouragement. They may need particular reassurance. Just as Nehemiah has initially motivated the people by sowing a vision among them of God's plans and purposes, so now he reminds both opponents and co-workers of those plans and assures them that what God has planned He will assuredly bring to fruition. It is easy for conflict to be presented as a clash of ideas or of preferences. The best way of heading this off is to refer people to God and what we know of Him, and to demonstrate that we are merely seeking to fall into line with what we know His will to be.

For others, change is threatening because it challenges their own spiritual complacency and undermines the defences they might have erected to keep God at a safe distance. The ways in which opposition is manifested are usually the same irrespective of its actual cause. Nehemiah variously experienced ridicule, character assassination, outbursts of anger, threats, attempts to trap him in compromise or to make him appear foolish, and attempts to distract him from the work to which he was committed. I can relate to most of those! Whatever the reason for this opposition being provoked, the impact upon us is usually the same. Our energy is sapped, our confidence can be rocked, self-doubt can creep in, we feel bruised and hurt and misunderstood, and we wonder if all this reengineering stuff is really worthwhile. Surely, we say, as we scan the "situations vacant" columns, there must be a church somewhere which is easier to lead!

As we explored in an earlier chapter, it takes some time for people to embrace change, and it is always worthwhile spending time helping such people deal with genuine reservations about the direction in which the church might be now going and coaxing them onwards. However, in my experience, it is rarely worthwhile to debate with those whose opposition is more visceral; those who are not simply having a rough ride on the transition journey, but who are adamantly opposed to what is happening and see it as their job to prevent change at all costs and, if necessary, take you down as part of the process.

It is very tempting to seek to defend ourselves in the face of attacks upon our character or motives and thereby to get sucked into fruitless argument. Nehemiah is a profound example of someone who refuses to be distracted from the course God has set for him or to waste his energies in unproductive disputes.[13] It is also worth noting that Nehemiah's instinctive turn in the face of such opposition is towards God. It is with God that he discusses the threats against him and the stuff he has to endure, and it is from God that he seeks resources with which to deal with his treatment at the hands of others.[14] The perverse truth about the experience of opposition is that God is well able to turn it to His advantage by causing it to become an avenue of spiritual growth for those of us who are on the receiving end of it.[15] As the medieval devotional writer Thomas à Kempis observes with his customary insight and wisdom:

> *It is good that at times we endure opposition, and that we are evilly and untruly judged when our actions and intentions are good, because often these experiences promote humility and protect us from vainglory.*

The way we deal with such opposition is important for a number of reasons. One of the clearest ways we can model true kingdom character is by the way we treat and respond to our opponents. There is something very winsome about handling opposition with dignity and grace, and by so modelling kingdom values we may well win more people over than by any amount of persuasive argument. Moreover, staying resolute and maintaining integrity in the face of opposition is important for other church members who are getting on board with the new vision and who themselves may also be the targets of the criticism of others. Nehemiah's self-discipline in the face of personal attack serves to rally the troops in Jerusalem and to reassure them in the face of fearful and bullying opponents.

At times when opposition is especially fierce we can encourage ourselves by dwelling on positive things that are happening. We can also spend time with encouraging people, whether inside or outside our own church (having a mentor or similar to whom you can unburden and with whom you can process stuff is enormously helpful at such times). Perhaps we could also take Jesus' advice and pray for those who persecute us![16]

## Demonic attack/harassment

The apostle Paul reminds the Ephesian Christians that our struggle for the kingdom is not primarily against human opposition but against hostile spiritual powers.[17] I am not of the school which attributes every difficulty to demonic agency (sometimes it really is just human fallenness and weakness which is to blame). However, it does pay to be aware of the fact that when we launch out in new kingdom enterprises we suddenly become a more significant threat to the kingdom of darkness and may find ourselves in a rather more focused spiritual battle.

The week in which I accepted the post of vicar of Saltburn was the week in which, for the first time in my life, I found myself, almost overnight, plunged into a depression which remained with me for the best part of a year and which was, at times, crippling in its intensity. Although there were a number of factors which probably had served to make me vulnerable to this (including ministering too much out of my own resources rather than God's, and the surfacing of some unhealed and unresolved emotional issues), it became clear in time that this was equally in no small part tied up with my appointment to Saltburn. Despite being prayed for by faithful and supportive friends, and despite spending time at a centre for healing, nothing seemed to shift the black cloud which hung over me.

As I cried out in desperation to God one Saturday evening, on my knees yet again in my study, I suddenly sensed Him speaking clearly in my spirit and instructing me to rebuke that spirit which had opposed ministers in Saltburn. As I stood up and took authority as He had commanded me, I sensed something lift, almost physically, from the very top of my head. The difference was instant and tangible. My shocked wife, upon seeing me, suggested that I looked as if I had just seen a ghost! I explained that I had just sent one packing!

I knew that my predecessor, a good and godly man, had moved on after a very short time in post, himself suffering from depression. His predecessor had been at the centre of a significant scandal over a sexual matter. I discovered that a minister from another church in the town had committed suicide in the recent past, and that other ministers had been plagued by various other difficulties and sadnesses. Those who had been at the sharp end of God's work had found themselves opposed and oppressed in all manner of ways and their effectiveness blunted.

We do well to be alert to the reality of the spiritual struggle in which we are engaged. The church of Jesus Christ in the power of the Spirit is a source of terror to the forces of darkness. They have to give way before it. When faced with significant threat to their influence or power, when confronted with the prospect of light coming in a new way to dispel the darkness, then they do what little they can to prevent or hinder the work of God's people. As Guy Chevreau so helpfully points out,[18] the work of Satan and his forces against God's people is far more one of *harassment* than of warfare. Harassment can be severe and fairly crippling for a time (as I discovered), but that is really all that it is.

The reality is that there is little if anything our adversaries can actually do to prevent the progress of God's work, as the power and authority of God is so overwhelmingly superior to anything that the opposition can bring against it. All that the demons are ever able to do when confronted by Jesus is to cry out in fear of their imminent destruction.[19] The apostle John who saw all this at first hand reminds us that "greater is He who is in you than he who is in the world",[20] while Jesus asserts quite clearly that He will build His church and that the gates of hell cannot prevail against it.[21] Gates are not, by the way (and contrary to some implicit theologies), offensive weapons. This picture that Jesus paints is of the church advancing, just as He did during His earthly ministry, and of darkness having to give way before it.

The earthly opponents of Nehemiah (Sanballat, Tobiah, Geshem, and others) behave in many ways akin to demonic sources of opposition, and illustrate the manner in which such opposition confronts us. They deal primarily in threats, in the cultivation of fear, in attempts to distract God's people from the task in hand, to preoccupy them with lesser concerns. They prey on insecurities and weaknesses, amplifying them in the minds of those who are being subjected to attack. Although this harassment is potent, it is not actually backed up with any substantial action. When the threats prove to be ineffectual against someone so resolute and so confident in God as is Nehemiah, they evaporate. Those issuing them fade away, their actual power revealed as being insubstantial. How are we called to act in the light of this spiritual battle?

We need to exercise proper discernment, recognizing the spiritual nature of the struggle in which we are engaged. Let me stress that I think it fruitless, unproductive, and actually playing into the enemy's hands by giving him overmuch attention, to go sniffing around for any lurking demons in our churches and communities. However, I do think that it is sensible to be alert to signs of demonic activity and influence, and to recognize opposition which seems to have more than merely a human root to it. Repeated patterns of unhealthy behaviour, deep-seated resistance to spiritual life, an emotional attachment to values which are contrary to gospel values, the kind of personal difficulties or depression which come at you out of the blue such as I experienced in Saltburn – all these may well indicate the presence of some demonic influence.

In one particular church for which I once had responsibility, we began to be concerned about a meanness of spirit and a lack of generosity at the heart of the church, and also a resistance to the authority of properly appointed leadership on the part of some long-standing church members. The church had been built in the last century by a local industrialist for his workers to attend. However, it had been built on a shoestring budget and everything about the building had something of a cost-cutting feel to it. Moreover, for the first few years of its existence, the church had been independent of wider church structures and was only subsequently brought under the authority of a local parish. As we prayed over some of the issues which we felt were holding back ministry in that church, we began to suspect that the roots may lie in the poverty spirit out of which the church was built and the independent spirit which defined its early years. Along with a handful of leaders, I spent an evening praying round the building, asserting the lordship of Jesus over the life and ministry of the church, giving the church "back" to Jesus, and rebuking both poverty and independence, and affirming generosity and obedience over the church.

The result was quite dramatic. The whole outlook of the church changed from that moment forward as it began to be suffused by warmth and generosity. Today that fellowship is unrecognizable from what it once was, not only in terms of physical appearance, but also in its spiritual identity. It is now a place where people are growing in faith and where, in recent years, a number of people have been brought to a living faith in Christ. It is well worth doing a similar exercise with the church for which you have concern, affirming what is good about its past, repenting of what has been wrong, and asserting the authority and lordship of Jesus over its future.

## Disappointment

The course of leadership is rarely straightforward. Every leader will face disappointments along the way. These are the things which often have the greatest capacity to knock the wind out of us. One of the chapters in the Bible which, somewhat perversely, encourages me more than most is 2 Corinthians 4. This is the chapter in which, in the space of sixteen verses, the apostle Paul twice asserts that, despite huge levels of difficulty, "We do not lose heart." I am pretty sure that anyone who repeats this phrase twice in such a short space of time is probably someone who is very close to the point of actually losing heart! Not only does this remind us that if this was the experience of so remarkable a leader as Paul it will surely be ours too, but also that there is no shame in feeling this way about whatever it is we are going through.

Usually it is *people* who cause us the greatest and most painful disappointment. Perhaps we have invested a good deal in someone who has shown great promise and who has made great strides forward in discipleship. Perhaps we have taken risks with them and entrusted significant levels of responsibility to them. Perhaps they have now let us down, begun to compromise in key areas of life, even fallen away from faith altogether. Not only does the time and effort we invested in them seem to have been to some extent wasted, but perhaps others are now suggesting that we showed poor judgment in ever considering such a person for leadership in the first place.

One of the most haunting verses in the entire New Testament must be 2 Timothy 1:15 where Paul writes to Timothy, "You are aware of the fact that all who are in Asia turned away from me."[22] There is no guarantee that all the ground we see gained for the kingdom in the lives of everyone will actually be held in the long term. At painful times like these, it is vital that we celebrate the lasting fruit that we do see, even if it appears a bit sparse, and imperative that we do not allow real disappointments to hold us back from continuing to invest in other people.

Sometimes our disappointment is with ourselves. All of us are flawed and imperfect people. We have mixed motives and possess characters which are still being formed into the likeness of Christ. We will, each of us, in moments of frustration or annoyance, say things in a manner we might subsequently regret. We will go through times when we fear that we might have blown our capacity to lead others. We will make decisions that we grow to see as unwise.

The Bible offers great encouragement for those who realize our own weaknesses. God specializes in using people who do not have what it takes, and in rescuing and restoring those who foul up. Few will experience the depth of disappointment that the apostle Peter went through after failing on all the promises he had so recently made to Jesus and after the disgrace of being found wanting when given opportunity to stand with Jesus after His arrest. After three times denying any knowledge of his friend, Peter, Luke tells us, goes out and weeps bitterly.[23] One of the loveliest narratives in the whole of Scripture is that[24] in which Jesus restores Peter and recommissions him for leadership and service in the church. When we feel most disappointed with our own failures and shortcomings we need to understand that Jesus is there to restore us, to re-establish us, and to put us back on course.

Often our personal disappointment is not so much over failures in our own character but is more to do with our performance as leaders. It's not difficult to beat ourselves up over what we do not see happening or over what we are failing to achieve. One of the easiest temptations into which to fall is that of comparing ourselves with others who are, apparently, doing a much better job than we are and whose ministry is obviously far more fruitful and successful. It is at times like this that we are most prone to push ourselves too hard or to strive inappropriately in a desperate attempt to stave off disappointment.

This is when we most need to remind ourselves that leadership truly is for the long haul and that a quick burst of frenetic sprinting will not only fail to produce the results for which we long but will also probably cause us to pull up with exhaustion. We need to hold on to the truth that God simply calls us to be faithful in our stewardship of the resources He has entrusted to us. We must understand that many factors, and not simply our own performance, contribute to the health and growth of our church. The social and spiritual climate in which we are operating, the level of Christian understanding among existing church members, levels of resistance to gospel ministry, and many other factors all serve to affect the pace of growth. Of course we have a part to play, and without careful leadership it is highly unlikely that a church will see any real growth at all. However, this is very different from holding ourselves exclusively responsible for the success or failure of the rate of progress in our church.

Sometimes, honestly, our disappointment is with God. I have no doubts as to what was the most painful day of my time in Saltburn. I was called into the local hospital very early one morning to discover that our lovely friend Carol, who had been undergoing some tests there, had very suddenly, and completely unexpectedly, died, having been suffering from an undiagnosed cancer. Not only was this a bitter personal loss of one of our closest friends, but Carol was our worship leader, one of our key people and absolutely central to so much of the life and ministry of our church. Just when we seemed to be building a strong ministry team and moving forward as a church, we had been dealt a serious body blow. I still remember driving back from the hospital and quite literally shouting my complaints to God. What did He think He was playing at letting this happen? Why Carol? I had a list of people whom I would have been very happy for Him to take, and she certainly wasn't on it!

Of course, when my emotions settled down, I completely understood that God wasn't directly responsible for Carol's death. But there will be times when we get to thinking that we would much prefer it if He allowed things to work out differently. Sometimes, rather like the people of Israel in exile, we may well resort to feeling that our ways are hidden from God,[25] that God is taken up with projects more important to Him than the one with which we are involved and has somehow taken His eye off the ball insofar as we are concerned.

Being at the very centre of God's will, having responded faithfully to His call, and having experienced His favour and blessing, is still no guarantee that everything will work out just as we had hoped. The context in which our ministry is worked out is a battleground. There will be ebbs and flows in the progress of the work. Sometimes, as in every battle, there will be casualties. What can never be in doubt is the final outcome of the war. The One in whose service we are enlisted has already won the decisive victory. All that He ultimately requires of us is that we stay faithful, that we persevere, and, like a long-distance runner – especially in the middle stages of the race when we would rather be anywhere other than this particular cold, wet, and muddy place – that we keep our focus on crossing the finishing line. What might be the keys to persevering and to making sure that we last the course? Here are four. Unsurprisingly, they are modelled by Nehemiah.

## 1. CULTIVATE A STRONG INNER LIFE

Those among my peers who excelled at distance running were those who had trained the hardest. They had developed deep inner reserves of physical and mental strength upon which to draw during the hardest part of races. The ability to last the leadership course is fuelled by having a life which is deeply rooted in God and which has learned how to be sustained by everything which He supplies. Nehemiah's response to challenges is always to go straight to God. When he first hears catastrophic news from Jerusalem,[26] he pours his heart out before God and begs for resources from Him. When people spread false reports about Nehemiah and seek to frighten him and disrupt the work of rebuilding, it is to God that Nehemiah turns to ask for strength.[27] It is an orientation around God's word that spurs Nehemiah on to social reform and to the removal from Jerusalem of practices which dishonour God and which compromise the faithfulness of God's people. A strong inner life is the ballast which holds Nehemiah secure and firm.

If we want to last the course we need to ensure that we are giving over adequate time to developing our own walk with God and to leading ourselves well in this way. As Bill Hybels reminds us:

> *Nobody – I mean nobody – can do the work of self-leadership for us. Every leader has to do this work alone, and it isn't easy. In fact, because it's such tough work most leaders avoid it. We would rather try to inspire or control the behaviour of others than face the rigorous work of self reflection and inner growth.[28]*

Wise leaders will always set aside adequate time for personal growth. As well as the discipline of daily personal prayer and reflection on Scripture, I have found it vital to set aside longer times to be with God, preferably away from my immediate work context. Each summer I usually go through the diary for the year ahead and block out a retreat week in the middle of the year, a reading week in early January, and a selection of monthly days away either for prayer or reading. I prioritize theological reading (usually of biblical theology or missiology) because I find it energizes me and keeps my mind fresh and alert to new ideas from God. When away on retreat, I tend to focus mainly on Bible meditation and on listening to God. This balance of feeding both mind and spirit has, over many years, sustained me through the highs and lows of ministry and has, by and large, kept me fresh and responsive to God. Paying attention to our inner life, to our walk with God, is that which helps us keep God firmly at the centre of all that we do and which enables us to gain strength from Him.

........................................................................

## 2. MAINTAIN PERSPECTIVE

There were plenty of times during my running career, usually just after the halfway point of a race, when I felt like giving up. The excitement of setting off and of jostling for early position had been left behind, the finish seemed way ahead and out of sight, there was loads of hard running to do, and things weren't turning out as I had hoped. The course was more demanding than I had reckoned, far too many people – whom I could never now hope of catching – had overtaken me, and I was running out of steam. Weren't there better ways of spending a Saturday morning? Sound familiar?

I imagine that the rebuilders of Jerusalem had more than a few moments when they found their enthusiasm waning and when they wondered if they had really bitten off more than they could chew. The task was immense, and, even though they quickly began to see some progress, I imagine that the dawning realization of the extent of the work that was still left to do began to sap their emotional energy. When opponents began to mock them and to spread rumours about the fomenting of a rebellion against the king,[29] and when, later, those same opponents began to plot physical violence against the people of Jerusalem,[30] perhaps their stamina began to ebb away. It certainly appears[31] that morale dropped and that people began to question their ability to complete the task.

There will be times in our church leadership when we feel like giving up. Whether it is the sheer scale of the task which still remains to be done, or the failure of nerve on the part of people who have journeyed with us thus far, or the pressure of opposition and the words of those who seek to undermine us – this can sometimes feel like a burden too great to bear. At different times in Saltburn, I had to live with the frustration that there were plenty of people who had not yet begun to own the new vision we were trying to see established and who seemed impervious to the work of the Spirit. Especially in the early years, I often had to encourage and spur on those who had embraced the vision but who now were alarmed at the hostility of friends and others within the church, and who were beginning to question the new initiatives we were bringing about. I heard, either directly or indirectly, of criticisms being voiced about me and the direction in which I was leading Emmanuel Church. This came from other local clergy, largely, I suspect, because my own ministry was taken as an implicit criticism of their own very traditional approaches to leadership.

Nehemiah never appears to look for encouragement and resourcing from either the affirmation of others or from the success of the work which he is overseeing, let alone from any acclaim for his ministry from other leaders. Time and again, he not only looks to God for his own encouragement, but he also directs others to God who has initiated this work and with whose purposes the work is integrally linked.[32] Nehemiah is able to sustain himself and others because he has filled his heart and mind with an understanding of God's nature and purposes. This is really what we mean by maintaining perspective – deliberately continuing to view reality from God's point of view. As Dallas Willard points out:

> *To live strongly and creatively in the Kingdom of*
> *God, we need to have firmly fixed in our minds*
> *what our future is to be like. We want to live fully in*
> *the Kingdom now and for that purpose our future*
> *must make sense to us. It must be something we can*

*now plan or make decisions in terms of with clarity and joyful anticipation. In this way, our future can be incorporated into our life now and our life now incorporated into our future.*[33]

This is the mindset of the apostle Paul, who insists that, despite grave difficulties and challenges, we do not lose heart but we fix our gaze on things which are eternal.[34] Our task is to keep uppermost in our minds that understanding of the purposes of God that first fired our imagination, the sense of God's call which brought us to the place in which we find ourselves. We must take heart from the assurance that God gives that He is truly working His purposes out and that our ministry has a small part to play in the unfolding of those great and sure purposes. Erwin McManus encourages us that:

*The natural outcome of being connected to God is being optimistic about the future. When this permeates a biblical community, optimism and enthusiasm prevail in the church. The church of Jesus Christ is always looking forward. It always believes in the promise of tomorrow and is never overwhelmed by the difficulty or even the failure of the present.*[35]

That might just put a spring in our step!

### 3. STAY FOCUSED

A few years after the collapse of the Communist regimes in Eastern Europe, I found myself, one summer, in Poland, speaking at an outreach among students. The event was taking place in the beautiful and remote Masury region where a group of over a hundred of us were camping by the side of one of the picturesque lakes so characteristic of the area. We spent our days swimming, sailing, playing sports, and chatting together, and then, as the evening drew in, we lit a bonfire and I talked about Jesus and about what it meant to follow Him. One day a group of us swam across the lake, a distance of a little over a mile, and then canoed back. It was idyllic.

A couple of days later, having ventured out towards the middle of the lake, I turned round to swim back. I suddenly realized that, right now, I was actually the only person out on the lake, everyone else having gone back to camp for lunch. It was a strange feeling. I was no more than a quarter of a mile from the shore, but I suddenly felt dreadfully exposed. What if I got cramp while swimming back? What if I didn't have the energy to cover the distance? Nobody would be there to help me. Although it was completely irrational (I had swum several times the distance without any difficulty a couple of days earlier, and I have never once in my life succumbed to cramp while swimming), I began to feel waves of panic sweeping over me and began to sense myself losing the ability to move my hands or legs properly.

As my life began to flash before me, and as the temptation grew to thrash out wildly (a sure way of both getting cramp and becoming exhausted!), I knew that I needed to get a grip on my imagination. So, I began to talk myself round, and to focus on the task in hand. I reminded myself that I was a strong enough swimmer to cover the distance back to shore many times over. I began to break the task down into manageable chunks and set myself the target of counting fifty strokes, and then another fifty. I deliberately looked away from the shore to which I was heading (it was the distance I had to travel that had initially alarmed me), and disciplined myself to look in that direction only after having completed each set of fifty strokes. Before long I was well into my stride and got back for lunch without any difficulty. Amazing, isn't it though, how easy it is to lose sight of the specific things we need to do in order to succeed at the task in hand. Amazing how easy it is to lose focus and to become distracted. And amazing how irrational fears and concerns, or simply a sense of isolation and exposure, can provoke such a loss of focus.

We have referred on several occasions in this book to Nehemiah's determination to maintain focus on the task in hand no matter what comes his way, and his refusal to be distracted from his primary purpose. His enemies tried all manner of ways to draw him away from the work. When threats and rumour-mongering failed to work, they resorted to more subtle and indirect approaches.[36]

All of us will have to deal with all manner of different things, each with the capacity to absorb our precious time and energies and to distract us from the primary task to which we have been called. We may well be tempted to do things which might win us favour with others or at least make them think less badly of us than they currently do. We may be flattered at invitations to get involved in other areas of ministry and service, some of which may well be worthwhile and, indeed, energizing for us, while others might be, honestly, a waste of time and a distraction from our primary calling. John Wimber used to remind us, "The main thing is to make sure that we keep the main thing, the main thing!" The apostle Paul memorably states his ambition as being to "press on to take hold of that for which Christ took hold of me".[37] Having an understanding that Christ has taken hold of us, that we are set apart in His mind for a particular purpose, helps maintain our sense of focus and keeps us from feeling either swamped by the scale of the task or tempted to waste our energies in ultimately fruitless exercises.

## 4. GET CONNECTED

Perseverance may be described as a corporate activity. It is pretty difficult to sustain leadership for the long haul all by ourselves. Those who last the course, those who prevail and who bear fruit, are those leaders who have learned the importance of keeping company with others who will help us stay focused on the task and remain hopeful in God. The writer to the Hebrews urges his audience not to neglect their practice of meeting together and, above all, to continue in the discipline of encouraging one another, spurring one another on and reminding one another of the faithfulness of God.[38] There will be plenty of people, both within the church and without, who, because of their outlook and behaviour, will sap enthusiasm and energy from us. Therefore, it is all the more vital to unearth people who will act as "fillers" rather than "drainers", who will be life-giving and encouraging, and be intentional about spending time with them.

In my experience, it takes a while to see a positive spiritual culture established in a church such that we feel resourced and nourished by the church which we lead. This has certainly eventually been the case with both the churches I have been privileged to lead, but in the days prior to this, I was heavily reliant on those beyond my own church family. Early on in our time in Saltburn we were blessed to make friends with another couple who were church planting in a neighbouring community. As well as valuing their friendship immensely, we used to agree to meet up on a monthly basis to talk through our respective leadership and ministry issues, to encourage each other, and to pray for one another. It was invaluable.

At the heart of the New Wine Movement is a network of small accountability groups, each consisting of around six to ten church leaders, and each of which meets for a couple of hours every four to six weeks. These groups use an adaptation of John Wesley's accountability questions which he devised for use among his Bands, focusing on areas such as character, personal walk with God, and faithfulness to kingdom values. Meetings consist of personal sharing around successes and failures in these key areas, encouragement especially in areas of difficulty, and then a good time spent praying for one another in the power of the Spirit. Meeting regularly with others who might be facing similar situations and challenges, and also with those who might be a little further ahead along the road, is enormously useful and strengthening. Joining a local New Wine Core Group,[39] or something similar, might be the best thing you could do, and will be a lifesaver for some.

## WHY WE RUN THE RACE

Sometimes, in the latter stages of a cross-country race, I did ask myself why I was putting myself through this ordeal... again! Of course, I must have enjoyed the experience enough to keep on coming back for more. It wasn't about success or accolades. I knew full well that I wasn't good enough ever to have a chance of winning a race. I did enjoy the idea of being part of a school sports team, and I did very much like the cross-country master who kept on selecting me. He was enthusiastic, always encouraging, and always at the finish line cheering us home. Part of the motivation to compete came from not wanting to let him down and to repay the trust and confidence he had shown in me.

It may be that we never quite see all our dreams and longings fulfilled, that we never see our visions come fully to fruition. It may be that our experience is unremittingly hard and frustrating. We feel sure that others would do a far better job than us. We may well find ourselves asking, why is it that we keep on doing this? I think I have kept on going simply because somebody picked me to run this race. The work in which I have been engaged has been God's appointment for me. There may well have been many others better equipped than I am to run this race. But He chose me, and I accepted the call. I am in the race until He tells me to stop or chooses me for a different one. Like Paul and Nehemiah, and others too countless to mention, I want to please the One who enlisted me. All that He requires from me is that I keep on going and refuse to give up. He, it seems, undertakes to do the rest. I keep on running, too, because He is cheering me on. It is not His place to run as I am called to run, but it is His commitment to coach and encourage me, to spur me on, to provide for me all the resources I need to do that which He has asked me to do.

And, finally, I suppose I keep on going because the race is worth running. The goal is important and glorious. The churches we lead or of which we are a part will always be flawed and an imperfect reflection of the church as it will one day be. But in the power of the Spirit they can become adequate reflections of the beauty and truth, the welcome and invitation, of God. They can begin to resemble the kind of communities God had in mind when He began to call out a people to fulfil His own unique purposes. As we continue to run the race, we will gradually begin to see the divine spark reignited in such communities and we will find ourselves agreeing with this glorious affirmation from Erwin McManus of what church can and should be:

*I am convinced that the local church can be a place where every believer experiences the fullness of life for which Jesus died and where every believer can experience healing and transformation. It can be a place where every believer can pray in such a way that history changes and where every believer can*

*die to himself and become a source of unbelievable*
*sacrifice and generosity. The church can become*
*a place where for every believer relationships*
*become the core value of life, helping the lonely*
*find acceptance and those without Christ experience*
*unconditional love.*[40]

## FURTHER READING

Guy Chevreau, *Our Eyes Fixed on Jesus*, Chichester: New Wine Ministries, 2006

Wayne Cordeiro, *The Divine Mentor*, Grand Rapids, MI: Bethany House, 2007

James Houston, *Prayer: The Transforming Friendship*, Oxford: Lion, 1989

Bill Johnson, *Strengthen Yourself in the Lord*, Shippensburg, PA: Destiny Image, 2007

# Questions For Group Study

The following Study Guide contains questions around the content of each of the book's eight chapters. I hope that these questions might provoke further reflection on the topics in hand for all readers and serve as a stimulus to acting upon the principles outlined in the different chapters. However, in compiling this section I have two groups of people particularly in mind.

Numerous leaders have been asking me for information about the coaching/mentoring groups I have run in recent years for leaders who find themselves in reengineering contexts. There seem to be rather a lot of church leaders who are hungry for help and wisdom in such situations. It may be that groups of such leaders who find themselves within travelling distance of each other could read the book, chapter by chapter, and then meet up to process these different principles and ideas, working out what they might mean in practice in their respective contexts, and forming a peer mentoring group together. The questions are designed to help such people apply these principles in a very practical way.

Some might find themselves in a local church whose overall leadership is fearful of change and in need of encouragement to allow things to move forward. Reading this book may well be prompting you to reflect on what you could do in order to bring such encouragement to your positional leaders. This study section, I hope, might help you work this out in the company of other people with similar longings and concerns.

## Chapter 1

### *Recovering Our Identity: The Church That God Has In Mind*

1. This chapter introduced us to several key biblical themes which inform and describe the nature and calling of the church (light to the nations, incarnation, servant of the Lord, body of Christ, missional people). How do each of these phrases help us understand who we are called to be as the church of Jesus Christ?

2. Can you think of other biblical images, titles, truths, etc., which also shed light on our identity and purpose as God's church?

3. What, according to these titles, do you think God intends to be our main priorities as a local church? How far does our own church express and organize its life around such priorities?

4. What do you think it means for the church to be a "sign and foretaste" of God's coming kingdom? What are the most important features of this kingdom that the church is called to express?

5. If Jesus were responsible for the shaping of the life and ministry of the church of which you are part, what elements do you think He might be most keen to change, and what might He be most likely to preserve?

6. What might we do in order to help our church grow increasingly into the likeness of the church that God has in mind? What might be the principal obstacles to be overcome if we are to see this come about?

7. Can you see any parallels between your own situation and that which confronted Nehemiah in Nehemiah 1? What might we learn from the way in which he approached the task before him? Are there particular lessons we might apply to our own context?

8. What has been the most significant thing you will take away from this study?

9. As a result of this session, what action do you think God is calling you to take?

Now spend some time praying for one another, asking God to strengthen us in the steps we feel called to take.

# Chapter 2

## *Moving Things Forward: Leadership As A Catalyst For Change*

1. How important do you think effective leadership is in the development and growth of healthy churches? Why?

2. Walter Wright suggests that:

   *If by leader we mean someone who holds a position of authority and responsibility, then every Christian is not a leader. But if by leader we mean a person who enters into relationship with another person to influence their behaviour, values or attitudes, then I would suggest that all Christians should be leaders. Or, perhaps, more accurately, all Christians should exercise leadership.*

   How far do you agree with this definition of leadership? How would you define and describe the nature of leadership?

3. How might it be possible to exercise leadership and influence in a local church without having any formal leadership position? How might God be calling you to exercise leadership influence for Him? What opportunities do you have to engage in such leadership?

4. What encouragement might you want to give to those who do not see themselves as "born" leaders or as not having any particular innate leadership gifts? How might such people be helped to exercise influence in the church and in the world?

5. *"Authentic leadership will always have a focus on moving things forward and is thus principally concerned with enabling change to come about."*
   How far do you agree with this statement? What particular factors shape your answer to this question?

6. In this chapter we suggest a number of characteristics of effective leadership. For each one, spend some time discussing:
   - what such a characteristic looks like in practice;
   - how strongly this characteristic is expressed in your own life and leadership;
   - what factors have been especially helpful in seeing this quality birthed and nurtured in your own life;
   - what steps you might take in order to grow in this specific quality.

7. Stephen Cottrell suggests that:
   *The most important quality in terms of day to day leadership is the willingness to recall the organisation to its primary vocation... The leader is the one who dares the whole organisation to stop for a minute and take time out to remember why they are there.*

   What practical things might a leader helpfully do in order to fulfil this particular leadership calling? In what ways are you currently prioritizing this calling and task?

8. What has been the most significant thing you will take away from this study?

9. As a result of this session, what action do you think God is calling you to take?

Now spend some time praying for one another, asking God to strengthen us in the steps we feel called to take.

## Chapter 3

### *Imagining The Future: Articulating Vision That Stirs The Heart*

1. How clear are you in terms of having a recognizable vision for the church of which you are a part?

2. Are there ways in which you feel your church might be helped by the wider ownership of a clear and compelling vision? Can you specify what these might be?

3. To what extent would you describe your leadership as reactive (responding to today's most pressing issue), and how far would you say you are able to be proactive, allowing your leadership to be shaped by a vision of where you feel God might want to lead the church?

4. What steps have you taken, and what steps might you take, in order to listen more effectively to God, to your context, and to others as you seek to formulate a clear vision for your own context?

5. Can you think of specific ways in which you might work with others to discern or to clarify a more coherent vision for the church in which you are involved? Who ought you to involve in this process, what particular steps ought you to take, and what exercises can you imagine might be most helpful for the formation of a clear corporate vision?

6. How widely would you say is your vision for your church owned by those who would see themselves as part of the church? What actions might you take in order to help others understand, embrace, and commit to such a vision?

7. What strikes you most from the ministry of Nehemiah and from the way in which he casts vision among the people of Jerusalem? Are there specific ways in which you might imitate his example?

8. In what area of discerning, articulating, and communicating vision do you most need help?

9. What has been the most significant thing you will take away from this study?

10. As a result of this session, what action do you think God is calling you to take?

Now spend some time praying for one another, asking God to strengthen us in the steps we feel called to take.

## Chapter 4
### *Holding On Tight: Leading Through Transitions*

1. What particular insights in this chapter did you find most helpful?

2. William Bridges describes transition as encompassing three distinct phases. Can you identify with this model of transition? Are there ways in which you have seen these three phases unfold in a transition which you have led? Does this understanding cast any light on your present experience of leading change in your church?

3. What skills might be required to lead a church through "The Neutral Zone"? What should be the major emphases of your leadership during this particular phase?

4. How might we learn to discern the appropriate pace at which change should be introduced and then seen through? What factors might influence this?

5. How do you respond to conflict? Are there ways in which you might learn to deal more constructively with conflict?

6. In this chapter we explore several "Do's" and "Don'ts" for leading through transition. Which of these practices do you find yourself pressing into instinctively? In which of these practices are you relatively weak? How might you grow in them?

7. Can you think of specific biblical narratives which shed light on and give encouragement to us as we lead through transitions?

8. What has been the most significant thing you will take away from this study?

9. As a result of this session, what action do you think God is calling you to take?

Now spend some time praying for one another, asking God to strengthen us in the steps we feel called to take.

## Chapter 5

### *Hosting God's Presence: Allowing The Spirit Freedom To Move*

1. What steps might I take in order to promote a greater expectancy among the members of my church in terms of encountering God in a more direct way?

2. What do I learn from the model and example of Jesus about what it means to work in partnership with God and to live in the power of the Spirit?

223

3. How can I model more completely to others what life in the Spirit looks like?

4. Are there ways in which I am restricting the freedom of the Spirit to work in my church? What specific issues do I feel are the most significant hindrances to the free movement of the Spirit in my church (e.g. fear of losing face, fear of others being disturbed, etc.)?

5. What steps might we take in order to give people in our church greater opportunity to encounter the presence of God's Spirit?

6. What barriers might need to be overcome in order to enable this to take place?

7. How good am I at giving space for testimony, for the telling of stories about ways in which people have encountered God and been impacted by Him? What opportunities could I create for this to take place in a more structured way in the life of our church?

8. What has been the most significant thing you will take away from this study?

9. As a result of this session, what action do you think God is calling you to take?

Now spend some time praying for one another, asking God to strengthen us in the steps we feel called to take.

## Chapter 6

### *Increasing Capacity: Growing And Developing Leaders*

1. How easy do you find it to resist the temptation simply to be a "doer of tasks" and rather to focus on being a "developer of people"?

2. What do you find most striking about Jesus' priorities for His own ministry? What implications might this have for the way in which we are called to exercise leadership today?

3. What steps might we take in order to create a climate in our church in which people might be encouraged and enabled to grow in personal discipleship?

4. We suggest a list of core attributes to look for as we seek to identify potential leaders. Look at each one in turn and reflect on what this attribute might look like in practice. Are there other core attributes which you would see as essential in any potential leader? Why do you see such an attribute as being important?

5. What might you put in place to develop and equip emerging leaders?

6. *"It is not the leader's job to do everything, but it is the leader's job to make sure that everything is done."* How far do you agree with this observation by John Wimber? What implications might it have for the way in which you conduct yourself as a leader and allocate your own personal resources?

7. What has been the most significant thing you will take away from this study?

8. As a result of this session, what action do you think God is calling you to take?

Now spend some time praying for one another, asking God to strengthen us in the steps we feel called to take.

## Chapter 7

### *Organizing For Growth: Developing Functional Structures*

1. Can you think of concrete ways in which dysfunctional structures actually hold back the capacity of your own church to fulfil its calling under God?

2. Christian Schwarz writes about the importance of removing as many as possible of the obstacles to church growth which we allow to proliferate in our churches. What are the particular hindrances to growth which you identify in the life of your own church? What steps might you take to deal with them?

3. How far are things in your church shaped by structures which were once shaped to achieve a positive purpose but which now effectively exercise a stranglehold on life?

4. Given the calling we have from God, if we were starting out from scratch, would we structure things according to our current pattern? What would we change? What prevents us from seeking to effect such changes?

5. What steps might we take in order to establish an effective structure of multiplying small groups? If we have a small group structure, is it accomplishing the purposes of forming missional disciples? If not, how might we develop it in order to see such a purpose achieved? What specific steps do we need to take?

6. How far is responsibility for ministry development in your church devolved to appropriate "heads of ministry areas"? Can you think of people whom God might be beginning to raise up as potential leaders of ministry areas? How might you develop them?

7. What steps are you taking to invest in existing leaders? What more might you do in order to develop them?

8. Would you describe your current public worship in church as an inspiring experience? What might be done in order to make it more inspiring and more of a vehicle through which others might encounter God?

9. What has been the most significant thing you will take away from this study?

10. As a result of this session, what action do you think God is calling you to take?

Now spend some time praying for one another, asking God to strengthen us in the steps we feel called to take.

## Chapter 8.

### *Staying The Course: Leadership For The Long Haul*

1. How easy do you find it to pace yourself in life and leadership? How frequently do you need to remind yourself that ministry is a marathon rather than a sprint? In what ways does the tendency to "sprint" manifest itself in your own life?

2. How easy do we find it to invest in things which may well not bear fruit in our own time as leader, but rather in that of our successor?

3. Why do you think that the New Testament writers celebrate perseverance almost more than any other virtue?

4. What specific challenges do you commonly face which threaten your own capacity to persevere?

5. How might we best deal with human opposition to change and development which we believe is in line

with the leading of God's Spirit? How does it help us to understand the specific roots of such opposition?

6. Can you think of ways in which some of the opposition you are currently facing, or may have faced in the past, might have a demonic root to it? How might we identify opposition as being demonic rather than as being simply human in its motivation? What strategies might you adopt in order to deal with such opposition?

7. Are there ways in which you are currently affected by disappointment? What impact does this have upon you?

8. What specific strategies might we adopt in order to enable us to sustain leadership for the long haul?

9. What steps might I take in order to develop a stronger inner life?

10. What strategies might I adopt in order to maintain perspective and to keep focused?

11. How intentional am I in connecting with others who might keep me spiritually sharp and focused on fulfilling God's call upon me? What more could I do in order to make sure that I prioritize cultivating relationship with such people?

12. What has been the most significant thing you will take away from this study?

13. As a result of this session, what action do you think God is calling you to take?

Now spend some time praying for one another, asking God to strengthen us in the steps we feel called to take.

# Notes

## Introduction

1. Bill Hybels, *Courageous Leadership*, Grand Rapids, MI: Zondervan, 2002, p. 12.

2. OECD figures have shown this to be particularly acute in the UK and some parts of Western Europe.

3. The World Health Organization has identified a global rise in depression and other mental health issues: http://www.who.int/mediacentre/factsheets/fs369/en/

4. The US has a particularly high percentage of the population in prison, and the UK has its largest ever prison population.

5. Quoted in a talk by Peter Brierley, from 2010 National Church Attendance Survey.

6. http://www.operationworld.org/hidden/evangelical-growth

7. Matthew 16:18

8. Luke 4:18–21

9. It was Bill Hybels (*Courageous Leadership*, p.153) who defined this leadership style clearly for me and helped me see that this was exactly the way God had wired me. Reengineering leaders are entrepreneurial to a degree and, as we shall see, rely on an ability to cast vision in order to get a task done, but they differ from classic church planters in that they are not starting completely from scratch.

"Re-engineering leaders love to patch up, tune up, and revitalize hurting organisations… When they find (something in need of overhaul) they start salivating. 'Would you look at that Kingdom train wreck,' they say. 'If I could get my hands on all that twisted metal, I know I could turn it into something great for God.'"

The classic biblical example of a reengineering leader is Nehemiah.

## 1. Recovering Our Identity: The Church That God Has In Mind

1. David Prior, *The Message of 1 Corinthians: Life in the Local Church* (The Bible Speaks Today), IVP, 1993, p. 196.

2. Alan Hirsch, *The Forgotten Ways: Reactivating the Missional Church*, Grand Rapids, MI: Brazos, 2007, p. 238.

3. Alan Roxburgh and Fred Romanuk, *The Missional Leader*, San Francisco: Jossey-Bass, 2006, p. xv.

4. Ann Morisey, *Beyond the Good Samaritan*, London: Mowbray, 1997, p. 3.

5. Nehemiah 1:4; 2:2

6. Genesis 12:2; 18:18

7. Isaiah 42:6; 60:1

8. Ezekiel 36:22–32

9. See http://www.tearfund.org/en/about_us/what_we_do_and_where/initiatives/umoja/ for further information

10. John 1:14, The Message

11. Isaiah 42:6–7; 61:1–3; cf. Luke 4:17–21

12. Mark 1:15, NIV

13. Mark 1:27

14. Mark 1:45; 2:15

15. Matthew 11:1–5

16. John 14:12

17. John 20:21

18. Acts 1:2 —This is the NASB translation, more accurate and more forceful than the NIV's rendering of εντειλαμενοσ as "giving instructions".

19. Acts 1:3

20. Acts 1:8

21. If the answer to our earlier question "would Jesus do things this way?" is in any way negative, perhaps it might be profitable to ask just why we think it might ever be legitimate for a church to espouse emphases, values, priorities, and structures that are in any way at variance with the ways in which Jesus might choose to order things?

22. In his introduction to the book, Luke refers to his earlier Gospel as an account of all that Jesus began to do and teach, the implication being that this second volume is an account of all He continued to do. This inference is made explicit in Acts 2:47 where the growth in the church that comes about through the apostolic ministry is described as "the Lord adding to their number day by day those who were being saved".

23. Acts 1:8

24. Acts 15

25. Alan Hirsch and Tim Catchim, *The Permanent Revolution: Apostolic Imagination and Practice for the 21st Century*, San Francisco: Jossey-Bass, 2012, p. 7.

## 2. Moving Things Forward: Leadership As A Catalyst For Change

1. Hybels, *Courageous Leadership*, p. 26

2. Richard Bolden, "What is Leadership?" *Leadership South West Research Report*, Exeter, 2004.

3. Robert Banks and Bernice M. Ledbetter, *Reviewing Leadership: A Christian Evaluation of Current Approaches*, Grand Rapids, MI: Baker Academic, 2004, p. 113.

4. In November 2014 amazon.com listed for sale over 157,000 books on the topic of leadership.

5. Richard Bolden, Beverley Hawkins et al., *Exploring Leadership: Individual, Organizational and Societal Perspectives*, Oxford: OUP, 2011, p. 4.

6. The Church of England, Church Growth Research Programme, *From Anecdote to Evidence*, 2014, pp. 10–11: www.churchgrowthresearch.org.uk/report

7. George Barna, *Leaders on Leadership*, Ventura, CA: Regal Books, 1997, p. 18.

8. Walter Wright, *Relational Leadership*, Carlisle: Paternoster Press, 2000, p. 2.

9. Norman Shawchuck and Roger Heuser, *Leading the Congregation*, Nashville, TN: Abingdon Press, 2010, p. 171.

10. See especially Exodus 1–20

11. See Judges 6:11 – 7:25

12. David's early career, and that of his predecessor Saul, is described in 1 Samuel.

13. See Nehemiah 2:16

14. Nehemiah 2:10, NASB

15. Warren Bennis and Burt Nanus, *Leaders*, New York: Collins, 2007.

16. Bennis and Nanus, *Leaders*, p. 25.

17. Nehemiah 1:10–11

18. Peter M. Senge, *The Fifth Discipline*, London: Random House, 2006, p. 335.

19. Mark 4:30–32

20. Mark 4:27

21. Matthew 13:33

22. 2 Corinthians 5:17

23. Matthew 28:19; Acts 1:8

24. E.g. Revelation 21:1ff

25. Ephesians 4:11

26. Hirsch and Catchim, *The Permanent Revolution*, Chapter 1.

27. Nehemiah 2:5

28. Revelation 21:5

29. *From Anecdote to Evidence*, p. 30. By contrast, according to the research, more than three quarters of clergy who say that they are better than most at motivating people, inspiring and generating enthusiasm to action, and who describe themselves as having a growth mindset and prioritize numerical growth, actually do lead growing churches.

30. Walter Wright has been an excellent exponent of this dimension to leadership and his *Relational Leadership*, Carlisle: Paternoster Press, 2000, is an especially helpful exposition of this.

31. Walter Wright, *Mentoring*, Milton Keynes: Paternoster Press, 2004.

32. A significant body of recent literature has drawn attention to the importance of the deployment of emotional intelligence as a vital factor in the establishment of resonant, as opposed to dissonant, leadership environments; e.g. Daniel Goleman, Richard Boyatzis and Annie McKee, *Primal Leadership*, Boston, MA: Harvard Business School Press, 2004; Rob Goffee and Gareth Jones, *Why Should Anyone be Led by You?*, Boston, MA: Harvard Business School Press, 2006.

33. Nehemiah 2:17, NASB

34. Nehemiah 4:23; 5:16

35. Nehemiah 5:14–15

36. Shawchuck and Heuser, *Leading the Congregation*, p. 23.

37. Parochial Church Council, the body responsible, along with the vicar, for governance in a local Anglican church.

38. Nehemiah 4:12–14

39. Nehemiah 6:1–11

40. Nehemiah 13

41. Stephen Cottrell, *Hit the Ground Kneeling*, London: Church House Publishing, 2008, pp. 29, 42.

42. Nehemiah 2:18–20; 6:16

43. Nehemiah 6:9; 13:22

## 3. Imagining The Future: Articulating Vision That Stirs The Heart

1. Matthew Richter, source unknown.

2. David Pytches, *Leadership for New Life,* London: Hodder & Stoughton, 1998, p. 57.

3. Michael Frost and Alan Hirsch, *The Shaping of Things to Come,* Baker, 2003.

4. Acts 3:19

5. Ezra 4

6. Hybels, *Courageous Leadership*, p. 29.

7. Wright, *Relational Leadership*, p. 82.

8. Wright, *Relational Leadership*, p. 82.

9. Nehemiah 2:17–18

10. Bennis and Nanus, *Leaders*, p. 82.

11. Shawchuck and Heuser, *Leading the Congregation*, p. 140.

12. James Kouzes and Barry Posner, *The Leadership Challenge*, San Francisco, CA: Jossey-Bass, 2012, p. 100.

13. Shawchuck and Heuser, *Leading the Congregation*, p. 148.

14. Nehemiah faces the challenge of distraction on a number of occasions, usually when his enemies seek to sidetrack him from the work or invite him to justify himself in the face of unfair and untrue allegations against him. His refusal to succumb to such challenges (e.g. Nehemiah 6:3) is fuelled by a clear and overriding sense of purpose and a resultant clear set of priorities.

15. George Verwer, *Out of the Comfort Zone*, Minneapolis, MN: Bethany House, 2000.

16. Bennis and Nanus, *Leaders*, pp. 88–89.

17. Shawchuck and Heuser, *Leading the Congregation*, p. 69.

18. Quoted in Hirsch and Catchim, *The Permanent Revolution,* p. 97.

19. This is exactly what Nehemiah is doing in explaining "how the hand of God had been favorable to me" (2:18, NASB).

20. Kouzes and Posner, *The Leadership Challenge*, p. 118.

21. See especially Nehemiah 1 where he is described as weeping, fasting, and praying, and seeking God over a period of time which must have lasted for several months.

22. Cottrell, *Hit the Ground Kneeling,* pp. 29, 31.

23. James Lawrence, *Growing Leaders,* Oxford: BRF, 2004, p. 210.

24. One or two "Vision Sundays" at the beginning of September, a further one at the beginning of January, and a Vicar's Report to the church in April at the Church Annual Meeting.

25. Donna Ladkin, *Rethinking Leadership,* Cheltenham: Edward Elgar, 2010, Chapter 6.

## 4. Holding On Tight: Leading Through Transitions

1. William Bridges, *Managing Transitions,* London: Nicholas Brealey, 2014, p. x.

2. Lawrence, *Growing Leaders,* p. 210.

3. Nehemiah 4:7–12

4. Bridges, *Managing Transitions*, pp. 4–5.

5. Senge, *The Fifth Discipline,* p. 335.

6. Bridges, *Managing Transitions*, p. 35.

7. Bridges, *Managing Transitions*, p. 37.

8. Nehemiah 4:14

9. Patrick Lencioni, *The Five Dysfunctions of a Team,* San Francisco, CA: Jossey-Bass, 2002.

10. Mike Bonem, *In Pursuit of Great and Godly Leadership: Tapping the Wisdom of the World for the Kingdom of God*, San Francisco, CA: Jossey-Bass, 2012, p. 197.

11. Senge, *The Fifth Discipline*, pp. 139ff.

12. Senge, *The Fifth Discipline*, p. 142.

13. Senge, *The Fifth Discipline*, p. 140.

## 5. Hosting God's Presence: Allowing The Spirit Freedom To Move

1. Brad Long, Paul Stokes and Cindy Strickler, *Growing the Church in the Power of the Holy Spirit,* Grand Rapids, MI: Zondervan, 2008, p. 19.

2. Andrew Murray, *The Full Blessing of Pentecost,* Basingstoke: Lakeland, 1984, pp. 9–10.

3. David Platt, *Radical,* Colorado Springs, CO: Multnomah, 2010, p. 50.

4. I have subsequently learned that it is far better to keep our eyes open at all times in order to be able to track what the Holy Spirit is doing as we pray for people. As we might reasonably expect a surgeon to keep her eyes open while operating on us, it is always

preferable for those who are ministering to others similarly to keep their eyes open and thus be able to respond to what God is doing.

5. 2 Corinthians 5:16, NLT

6. Zechariah 4:6

7. Acts 1:4–5

8. Long et al., *Growing the Church*, p. 65.

9. Hebrews 2:17, NASB

If we are in any doubt as to the absolute reality of Jesus' sharing our vulnerable human nature, then a reading of the accounts of Jesus' two most significant battles with temptation (Luke 4:1–13 and Luke 22:39–46) should serve to remind us that he was subject to exactly the same pressures and self-doubts as we ourselves, an experience which would have been alien to one who had not let go of his heavenly powers.

10. Matthew 3:13–17; Mark 1:9–11; Luke 3:21–22

11. Matthew 12:28

12. John 5:19–20

13. Mark 1:22, 27

14. Mark 9:14–29

15. Acts 4:29–31

16. Long et al., *Growing the Church*, p. 37.

17. Simon Western, *Leadership: A Critical Text*, London: Sage, 2008, p. 116.

18. There are now New Wine summer conferences in several other European nations in addition to those which take place in different locations throughout the UK and Ireland.

19. New Wine also run a whole host of other national and local resourcing events for church members, church leaders, and for those involved in various different ministries. Details may be found on the New Wine website www.new-wine.org

## 6. Increasing Capacity: Growing And Developing Leaders

1. Wright, *Relational Leadership*, pp. 135, 148.

2. Quoted by Bill Hybels.

3. Howard Snyder, quoted in Hirsch and Catchim, *The Permanent Revolution,* p. 73.

4. John C. Maxwell, *Developing the Leaders Around You*, Nashville, TN: Nelson, 1995

5. Mark 3:13–19

6. It is clear that, although the twelve are seen by Jesus as His closest lieutenants and entrusted with significant ministry (e.g. Luke 9:1ff), there are a much wider group of others associated with Him who are equally being trained and released into ministry (e.g. Luke 10:1ff).

7. E.g. Mark 1:16–20; 2:14

8. Matthew 4:19

9. E.g. Titus 1:6–9

10. Robert Murray McCheyne, Journal 2/10/1840.

11. Wright, *Relational Leadership*, p. 147.

12. Nehemiah 2:17

13. Nehemiah 2:18

14. This ministry, which is becoming increasingly widespread among local churches, consists of a small team of church members setting up a healing prayer station usually in the middle of a busy shopping area. It is a way of going out to those who might never darken the doorstep of a church building, offering to pray for them and seeking to extend God's love and blessing to them. More details can be found at http://healingonthestreets.com/

15. Bennis and Nanus, *Leaders*, p. 176.

16. 2 Timothy 2:2

17. Erwin McManus, *Uprising*, Nashville, TN: Thomas Nelson, 2003, p. 80.

18. Mark 1:36–37

19. Mark 5:37

20. Mark 6:7–13

21. Mark 6:30–32

22. Bill Hybels describes it as "the breakfast of champions".

23. Acts 9:27, NASB

24. Acts 11:25–26

25. E.g. 2 Timothy 1:6–7

26. E.g. 2 Timothy 2:14–26

27. Hybels, *Courageous Leadership*.

28. Ephesians 4:7

29. 1 Corinthians 12:7

30. Cottrell, *Hit the Ground Kneeling,* p. 48

31. Maxwell, *Developing the Leaders Around You,* p. 172.

## 7. Organizing For Growth: Developing Functional Structures

1. *Mission-Shaped Church*, Church House Publishing, 2004, p. 10.

2. Alan Hirsch, *The Forgotten Ways,* Grand Rapids, MI: Brazos Press, 2006, p. 23.

3. 1 Corinthians 3:6

4. E.g. Mark 4:27

5. The British version of the results of this research is published as *Natural Church Development Handbook*, 1996.

6. Christian Schwarz, *Natural Church Development Handbook*, BCGA, 1996, p. 10.

7. Quoted in W. Vaus, *Mere Theology, A Guide to the Thought of C. S. Lewis,* Downers Grove, IL: Intervarsity, 2004, p. 167.

8. Schwarz, *Natural Church Development Handbook*, pp. 28–29.

9. Schwarz, *Natural Church Development Handbook*, p. 33.

10. Ideally I would have liked it to continue together for at least twice that length of time.

11. LICC have produced a range of brilliantly helpful materials including, most recently, a course entitled *Fruitfulness on the Frontline*. Details of all their products and resources can be found at http://www.licc.org.uk/

12. The most helpful Christian exposition of this is to be found in Richard Rohr, *The Enneagram – A Christian Perspective*, Crossroad Publishing Co., 2002.

13. The foundational text in which Meredith Belbin expounds his understanding of team roles is *Management Teams*, Routledge, 2010. There are a whole host of other related resources and a wide variety of websites, all of which explain Belbin's ideas and offer suggestions for using them in individual team contexts.

14. Schwarz, *Natural Church Development Handbook,* p. 31.

## 8. Staying The Course: Leadership For The Long Haul

1. Erwin McManus, *Chasing Daylight,* Nashville, TN: Thomas Nelson, 2010, p. 185.

2. J. Oswald Sanders, source unknown.

3. 1 Corinthians 3:6, NASB

4. Mark 13:13

5. Colossians 1:11, NIV

6. 2 Thessalonians 3:5

7. 1 Timothy 6:11; 2 Timothy 3:10

8. Hebrews 12:1–3

9. 2 Timothy 3:12, NASB

10. John 16:33

11. Nehemiah 2:19–20

12. Ezra 4

13. Nehemiah 6:1–14

14. Nehemiah 4:4–5; 6:14

15. Cf. Romans 5:3–4

16. Matthew 5:44

17. Ephesians 6:12

18. Guy Chevreau, *Our Eyes Fixed on Jesus : A Sideways Look at Spiritual Warfare,* Chichester: New Wine Press, 2006, p. 78.

19. Mark 1:24; 5:7–10

20. 1 John 4:4, NASB

21. Matthew 16:18

22. NASB

23. Luke 22:62

24. John 21:15ff

25. Isaiah 40:27

26. Nehemiah 1:4ff

27. Nehemiah 6:9

28. Hybels, *Courageous Leadership*, Chapter 9.

29. Nehemiah 2:19

30. Nehemiah 4:8

31. Nehemiah 4:10–12

32. E.g. Nehemiah 2:20; 4:14

33. Dallas Willard, *The Divine Conspiracy,* London: Fount, 1998, p. 410.

34. 2 Corinthians 4:16–18

35. McManus, *An Unstoppable Force*, p. 162.

36. E.g. Nehemiah 6:1–19

37. Philippians 3:12, NIV

38. Hebrews 10:23–25

39. Details of these and other local and national New Wine Network activities, events, and other resources, can be obtained from the New Wine website: http://www.new-wine.org/

40. McManus, *An Unstoppable Force,* p. 212